George Bernard Shaw

George Bernard Shaw

by OLIVIA COOLIDGE

HOUGHTON MIFFLIN COMPANY BOSTON / 1968

We should like to credit the following sources for the photographs that appear in the book: The Bettmann Archive, Inc. for photographs on pages 39, 43, 61, 68 left, 71, 102, 115, 133, and 194; Culver Pictures, Inc. for the frontispiece photograph and those on pages 168, 199, 202, 213, and 226; Wide World Photos for pages 183, 184, 191, and 211; The Keystone Press for pages 147 and 206; The Radio Times Hulton Picture Library for pages 68 right and 90; The Mander and Mitchenson Theater Collection for pages 123 and 154; Hutchinson and Company (Publishers) Ltd. for photographs on pages 7, 12, and 16 taken from *Jesting Apostle: The Life of Bernard Shaw* by Stephen Winsten; and Jaeger Company Shops Ltd. for the photograph on page 31. Front jacket photo is courtesy of The Bettmann Archive, Inc. Back jacket photo is courtesy of The University of North Carolina Library.

CONTENTS

Introduction

Wᴴᴬᵀ ɪѕ an Irishman? Bernard Shaw's family was not Catholic; and as far as is known he had not a drop of Celtic blood, his ancestors being English or Lowland Scots, though they had resided in Ireland for a good many generations. His upbringing, insofar as he may be said to have had any, was directed towards keeping him separate from the great mass of his countrymen. His very accent rubbed off with the years until in old age it was not noticeable. Two things he may be said to have brought from Dublin and retained all his life: his courtly manners and the nature of his wit — though his actual sense of humor was an inheritance from his father.

These may seem rather small reasons for calling a man Irish, and Shaw was clearly puzzled himself about what his Irishness was. He had no great love for the island, never went back there except at the urging of his wife, and held firmly to the view that the best thing that could happen to every Irishman was to get out of the country. Nor was he ever popular there when he was famous. His thinking was too unconventional, and he totally lacked Irish romantic national feelings. On the whole, Shaw was inclined to say that the effect of the climate on his ancestors had made them Irish in spite of themselves. It was a theory which could only be maintained by somebody living in England, since none but the English would appreciate the rather fine distinction between Irish weather and their own. No, Shaw was Irish simply and solely because he felt he was.

He was never English, but it was about the English that he cared. It was at the English he mocked, it was English institutions that he spent his life in trying to reform, it was in the English that he exposed stupidities which an exceptional man must needs discern in other people. The nineteenth century, the Industrial Revolution, even capitalism itself were all to him English. England was his reluctant ward, his battleground, his hope or despair for the future, and the only country in the world he wanted to live in.

What made him an exceptional man in England was precisely the fact that he felt foreign, never hampered by English tradition or sentimental feeling. As the son of a down-at-heels gentleman, he was thrust out into the world at sixteen to earn a pittance, so that he had no experience of the comfortable side of the capitalistic system. Wretchedly educated for five years in indifferent schools, he missed altogether the classical discipline which was the intellectual prop of the regime. Neglected by his parents and left to do or think what he pleased, he was never emotionally attached to a system of moral values which was growing out of date as he came of age. Moving to England at the age of twenty, and struggling for nine years to find his niche in London, he was thus extraordinarily detached from the world he lived in. It was this detachment, enabling him to take a fresh view, which he called being Irish.

For his genius he had no explanation at all. His parents were the last people to have produced such a son, and it is not enough to say that his father had a sense of humor and his mother a capacity for living in a world of her imagination. He thought of himself almost as a medium. Some power in him drove him to write; words flowed out of him not without effort and yet in a certain vital sense unplanned, since he did not always perceive the direction in which his thought was flowing till it got there. Perhaps for this reason he tended to write or talk too much, since brilliant ideas were not dominated throughout by clear conception of the end to which they ought to be directed.

It was almost a source of confusion that he was so richly gifted. He was equally capable of slapdash humor and profound thought backed up with serious knowledge. His imagination had an extraordinary power of penetrating motives. Generally speaking, his plots were careless affairs, mere vehicles for the sugar and spice of his work. No one, however, has excelled him in the excitement which can be created by a clash of ideas. No one has brought so many important ideas to the stage or displayed trite situations from so many different and unexpected angles.

No one either has had a more wide-ranging effect on the values of his time in politics, morals, custom, and religion. To be sure, his was a long life, and there were within it many other forces at work, as the nineteenth century gave way to the twentieth. Notwithstanding, for many years he led the way in the Fabian Society and in a series of immortal dramas. Toward the end of his life, he was asked which of the two had been more important, and he chose the plays. He was right. The Fabian Society still attempts to better the world; but it is different now, and *Fabian Essays* is little more than a record of the past. But times may change, while Major Barbara, Joan, Caesar, and Lavinia do not. Some problems which Shaw has tackled may become outdated, but a great play in which imagination treats a lofty subject is enduring.

1856–1876

Dublin

"I WILL," said Lucinda Elizabeth Gurley, defiantly conscious that her elders thought she was making a mistake. Lucinda Elizabeth, though she was not marrying for love, held to the opinion that she had chosen the least of possible evils. In the end, she may have proved right.

Lucinda Elizabeth was called plain Bessie at home, and the contrast between her pretentious name and its unromantic contraction expressed very neatly the difference between her real and her imagined social value. The discrepancy was not Lucinda Elizabeth's fault. The girl was pretty, since an adolescent roundness concealed for the present her hard, determined jaw and the thin gash of her mouth. She tinkled on the piano and sang, with the advantage over other genteel girls that she really was musical. She recited a couple of the fables of La Fontaine in well-drilled French. She dressed and spoke like a lady. But her father was a sporting Irish squireen who lived by sponging and whose only pretensions to gentility were the possession of mortgaged estates and his Protes-

tant religion. Motherless, Lucinda Elizabeth owed education and manners to her aunt.

Miss Ellen Whitcroft, a spinster of modest wealth,
had a hunchback, which had prevented her from making
an acceptable marriage. The loss had been the greater
because she was conscious that her claims to be a gentle-
woman needed reinforcing. Her father had been a pawnbroker in Dublin. To be sure, he had not managed the
shop in person, but had bought himself an estate and
married into the county. All the same, Miss Whitcroft's
money had been gained in retail trade of a not very repu-
table sort. She was determined that her niece should
wipe out this disgrace by making a handsome match. To
this end, she had given Lucinda Elizabeth an education
which fitted her for nothing unless she could attract some
baronet's eye. Gentility was reinforced in Miss Whitcroft
by a stern, evangelical religion which had disgusted Lucinda Elizabeth by its severity. At seventeen, she was
already in revolt. The girl had the common sense to see
that her aunt's ambitions were impracticable. Miss Whitcroft did not go much into society and, even had she done
so, her niece and probable heir was no great catch. Lucinda Elizabeth understood that her prospects were
modest.

When Lucinda was seventeen, her disreputable father
decided to marry again. His choice did not commend
itself to his first wife's relatives, from whom he had bor-
rowed heavily. In fact, Gurley thought it wiser not to let
them know of the coming event. He made, however, the
mistake of telling his daughter who, in all innocence,

informed her aunt. News of the affair got out, with the result that Gurley, going out on his wedding day to buy himself a pair of gloves, was arrested for debt at the instance of his brother-in-law. The incident merely delayed the match. It also inflamed the bridegroom's temper against Lucinda Elizabeth at the very moment when she was finding her aunt intolerable. She had hoped a stepmother would make it possible for her to return to her father's home, despite its drawbacks. This escape being now cut off, her only alternative was marriage. An offer did come her way. She looked at it carefully, and she coolly said yes. George Carr Shaw to her was merely a refuge from relatives she could no longer live with.

No one was angrier than Miss Whitcroft. Her chagrin was all the greater because she had permitted George Shaw to take her niece about. What else was she to do? It was obvious that Lucinda Elizabeth must be seen in public if she was to catch the eye. But until she had done so, Miss Whitcroft was unwilling to trust her in company with ineligible suitors. In her difficulty, George Shaw had seemed a godsend. He was forty, for one thing, far too old to attract seventeen. Besides, he was so ineffective, so devoid of dash and enterprise that it had never occurred to Miss Whitcroft either that he would propose or that Lucinda would have him.

Miss Whitcroft proved wide of the mark. George Carr Shaw was a little man, and he squinted; but he was not ill-looking, the possessor of a fine, spreading beard. He dressed like a gentleman in business suit and watch chain. His manners were pleasant and gentle. He had a small income. Lucinda Elizabeth, deliberately kept ignorant of practical matters, had not the faintest idea of the value of money.

George Carr Shaw, like his intended bride, was a member of the Irish Protestant Ascendancy, descended from one of the groups of English and Scots who had settled in Ireland after the time of Cromwell. He was a gentleman by virtue of that fact, and he had received an education which had improved his manners rather than his mind. As one of eleven children, he had been inadequately prepared for life, which he faced without training or profession of any kind. Luckily for him, the Shaws were well connected. Sir Robert Shaw, baronet, of Bushy Park outside Dublin, was his second cousin. There was influence enough to get George Shaw a position connected with the Dublin law courts which he was able to hold without the slightest knowledge of law. Before he had met Lucinda Elizabeth, reform had swept away this useless job, compensating its holder with a pension of sixty pounds a year for life. It was largely on this pension that Lucinda Elizabeth in her innocence proposed to live.

Miss Whitcroft raged, and well she may have done so. Her niece, however, was fortified against her remarks in advance. She preferred to believe George Shaw, who was optimistic. The fact was, he was entering on a business deal with which he had not troubled his fiancée's pretty head. He had commuted his pension for an immediate cash bonus of five hundred pounds with which he was buying a share in a flour mill just outside Dublin, going into the business with a partner who, like himself, had neither experience nor aptitude.

"He drinks!" pronounced Miss Whitcroft in utter contempt. Lucinda at last was taken aback. She questioned George Shaw in real concern. He assured her with simple conviction that he had a lifelong hatred of liquor. He did not add that he also had a lifelong weakness for it.

Such was the match that Lucinda Elizabeth made, flying in the face of her relations. Miss Whitcroft was so incensed that she left her money elsewhere, endowing Lucinda Elizabeth with nothing except some IOU's signed by her father which had been given into the girl's possession earlier. It was hardly likely that Lucinda could have extracted anything from the tough and wily old man, but she might possibly have put in a claim against his estate when he died. Innocently she took the documents to him and asked him what she ought to do with them. "Throw them in the fire, my dear," replied the old wretch, gleefully suiting the action to the word. Thus ended Lucinda Elizabeth's expectations from her aunt.

The married pair honeymooned in Liverpool, which seems a strange choice of location. It was a strange honeymoon, too. Lucinda Elizabeth was young and determined to make the best of the life she had chosen. But her courage was broken by the discovery that the back of their wardrobe was full of empty bottles. Her aunt had been right after all. George Shaw was a drunkard.

She was alone when she faced this crisis — alone in a strange town and a foreign country. Her instinct was to get away, but how? She was not qualified to earn her living in any respectable fashion. The best she could think of was to go down to the docks and get a berth as stewardess. No doubt she had noticed that there were such beings on her voyage over.

Lucinda Elizabeth actually set out. But the appearance of a young lady by herself on the streets of Liverpool was fraught with danger, most especially down by the docks. Held up by some rowdies, Lucinda Elizabeth escaped unharmed, but in a panic. Desperately she retraced her steps. She had learned there are some things even worse than being married to a drunkard.

Lucinda Elizabeth had made her bed, and now she must lie on it. In actual fact, her situation, though wretched enough, was not quite desperate. For her husband she had nothing left but cool contempt. She did not hate him, but wrote him off as the merest cipher. Of other society she saw almost none. George Carr Shaw was one of those unfortunate tipplers who loathe themselves for their weakness. He was not even good company in his cups. The grand relatives at Bushy Park, though they approved of Lucinda, could not stomach her husband at family parties. Other members of the family followed their example. Lucinda Elizabeth, resenting the insult to herself, if not to her husband, had words with some of the ladies. The George Carr Shaws were soon invited nowhere.

Their drab house in a dreary district was shortly enlivened by children: Lucy Carr Shaw, Eleanor Agnes Shaw, and finally George Bernard Shaw in 1856. George Carr

Shaw was always in debt, and the family lived meanly; but they did not quite go under. He still wore his business suit and displayed his watch chain. She preserved her ladylike manners and superior air. Illiterate Dublin servant maids were cheap. Eight pounds a year and bed and board would buy one. There was a housemaid and what was called a nurse in the basement kitchen where the babies were casually brought up on bread and butter, stew, strong tea, and half-rotten potatoes.

Lucinda Elizabeth cared little for her daughters and, seemingly, nothing for her son. They were children of their ne'er-do-well father rather than her own. In any case the strictness of her upbringing had given her a horror of imposing discipline. The children were left to the nursemaids, who took their charges to visit their own friends in the slums or dumped them down in some bar

Shaw's birthplace in Dublin

while they had a chat and a drink. Slum conditions were horrifying to young George Bernard, a sensitive child; and they may be said to have marked his character for life. His mother, however, hardly knew whether he was in the house or outside it.

It was a loveless household. Young George Bernard, who was called Sonny at this stage, had been disposed to make a hero of his Papa, whose beard was still imposing, and whose sardonic sense of humor appealed to his offspring. One day, however, Papa took the child for a walk and in the course of it made believe to throw him in the canal. There was some horseplay, and Sonny conceived a terrible suspicion.

"You know, Mama," he whispered in a burst of confidence when he got home, "I think Papa is *drunk!*"

"Ah, when is he anything else?" retorted Lucinda Elizabeth in wearily indifferent tones which utterly killed Sonny's illusions. Such was the shock he felt that, looking back on it in old age, he almost wondered how he had dared feel deeply since.

The family life of the Shaws, though bleak, was not precisely unhappy. Lucinda might be indifferent; she was never unkind. She did not nag or quarrel with her husband. Between his bouts of drinking and repentance, George Shaw was not bad company. He had a peculiar sense of humor which delighted in anticlimax. Once he took Sonny swimming and lectured on the advantages of learning the art. "When I was fourteen," he said, "my knowledge of swimming enabled me to save your uncle Robert's life."

The boy was deeply impressed. Yielding to an impulse to spoil his own effect, the father stooped and added in a confidential whisper, "And to tell you the truth I was never so sorry for anything in my life afterwards." He plunged into the sea, enjoyed his swim, and chuckled over his wit the whole way home.

Such a man could now and again be entertaining. Sonny's childhood was also enlivened by the regular visits of an uncle. Walter Gurley had been sent to "the Eton of Ireland," where he had received a thorough grounding in drunkenness and vice. He took these habits with him to college, but he had some native ability, too; and in the course of time he became a doctor. He was by now the medical man on a merchant ship and was steady enough for the length of a voyage. When he got back to Dublin he had his fling. During these periods he made his home with the Shaws, who no doubt welcomed his money. Walter Gurley was no such guilty drinker as George Carr Shaw. On the contrary, he was a full-blooded man who had a good time in his own way and was frank about his experiences to a point where his conversation was unprintable. Curiously enough, his stories did young Sonny no harm and may have done some good, in that they enabled him to take his father's weakness less seriously. It was in company with Walter Gurley that the boy stood roaring with laughter as his father, trying to get through a gate with a goose under one arm and a ham under the other, mashed his top hat to ruin against a stone wall. "If you cannot get rid of the family skeleton," he commented later, "you may as well make it dance."

Walter Gurley, in fact, was a jolly man and fond of young Sonny, for whose edification he recounted Bible stories, always giving them a disreputable twist not intended by their authors. These tales were often capped by the humor of Sonny's father. The boy did go to Sunday school, but merely because it was right in his father's position that he should. Shaw and Lucinda avoided church. After a while, even the celebration of Christmas was given up; and Lucinda Elizabeth decided she was an atheist. At twelve years old, Sonny thought that he was, too.

Meanwhile, the rigid distinctions of Dublin society had fastened their iron grip on the boy from his earliest years. One day he bought a pennyworth of candy which the shopkeeper screwed up in a page of the Bible torn out for wrapping. Such was the child's shock at this sacrilege that he wondered why fire did not come down from Heaven to punish the wicked act. All the same, he took the sweets and ate them, reflecting that the shopkeeper was a Catholic and would go to hell in any case. Nor was it possible to feel sorry for him, since he was no gentleman.

A claim to gentility was far more serious in this small minority group than heartfelt religion. George Carr Shaw found his boy playing with the son of the owner of a hardware store. He called Sonny in for a little chat, explaining that wholesale traders like himself might be gentlemen, but shopkeepers were not people they could associate with. By the time Sonny was twelve, he well understood that his father's tailor, who had a yacht and could send his son to college, was not fit company for a miller who was behind with his bills, never read a book, and was always muddled by his simple accounts. The boy was conscious that such distinctions were absurd, but he accepted them as a part of existence.

Despite her deficiencies as a mother, Lucinda Elizabeth exercised one positive influence on her aimless household. Looking about for an interest on which she could expend her untapped energies, Lucinda Elizabeth had found herself in music. She happened to have a pure, clear mezzo-soprano voice; and there was in Dublin an impresario and voice trainer of parts called John George Vandaleur Lee. Lee had a system of voice production which, he claimed, superseded all systems currently in use. He even promised to preserve the purity of a properly trained voice into old age and performed this miracle in the case of Lucinda Elizabeth, who was his perfect pupil. Gifted by nature, and having no other occupations to eat up her time, she was ready not merely to master Lee's voice techniques, but to make an intensive study of music. Besides giving voice lessons, Lee put on concerts and opera, in part to display the talents of his pupils. Lucinda Elizabeth sang leading roles, copied orchestral parts, scored songs, led choruses, accompanied groups at the family piano, and even undertook to give voice lessons to beginners under Lee's direction.

It is difficult to overestimate the contribution made by this passion of Lucinda Elizabeth to the family atmosphere. For one thing, it soon transpired that the possessors of fine voices in the Dublin musical world were not

Lee surrounded by his disciples. Lucinda Elizabeth Shaw is on extreme left, George Shaw on extreme right.

all gentlefolk. Some of them were even Roman Catholics who, besides being unpresentable, were bound for hell. More remarkable still, the Catholic chapels were places where good music was being sung. They needed soloists; and where music was concerned, Lucinda Elizabeth had no scruples. On Sonny faint glimmerings began to dawn of what one might describe as education.

It was too much to expect that Lucinda Elizabeth would pay attention to her children's musical training unless they happened to be specially gifted. In the event, Lucy, blond and prettyish, proved to have a voice. Red-headed

Agnes and carroty-haired young George Bernard were welcome to strum on the piano when it was vacant, join in choruses, or listen to endless practice and rehearsals. Luckily music was a subject that never bored the Shaws. George Carr himself had a trombone and joined with a group of respectable gentlemen in giving free outdoor concerts on occasional Sundays. Sonny was welcome to experiment with his father's instrument, and he smashed it. No one considered the expense of an instrument for him or music lessons. It hardly mattered. His whole family life was an education in music.

Vandaleur Lee was an odd little man with a bad limp, sharp features, a vivacious expression, and a mop of black hair which looked as though it were a wig. He had great vitality and strong opinions, which were not entirely confined to matters of music. As a bachelor, he had shared a home with an invalid brother, who presently died. Thereupon, Lee proposed to Lucinda Elizabeth that he and the Shaws join forces. Since he gave private lessons at home, he absolutely needed a respectable house and a good address, though his wants would be satisfied by a bedroom and a music room. With his financial assistance, it would be possible for the Shaws to manage his establishment. In effect, they moved into comfortable quarters, and Lee gained a housekeeper and all the attention of his leading lady, secretary, assistant, and star pupil. It was only natural that the influence of George Carr Shaw over his family, which was already negligible, declined still further. Lucinda Elizabeth, however, was not in love with Lee. She had done with such emotions once and for all. She merely permitted him to dominate her musical life and also her household.

In this way, yet a third father-figure entered young Sonny's world. He was not fond of Lee, who had no experience or understanding of children. He could not, however, fail to be influenced by him. In particular, Lee was a health faddist who taught the family to eat brown bread and keep their windows open. He had a great contempt for doctors and proved his point by pulling Lucinda Elizabeth through a serious illness. But the greatest debt the boy owed to Lee was the opportunity to get out of Dublin streets and run wild in the country. Lee bought and made over to the Shaws a summer cottage outside Dublin with a marvelous view of the bay. Here a boy who was not athletic and lived very much in his own dreamworld could wander as he pleased, not missing his companions in the relief of getting away from his Dublin school.

In later life, Bernard Shaw was unable to regard schools as anything but prisons in which boys were shut up to keep them out of the way. His own experience of them was mercifully brief. Until eleven, he had lessons from his sisters' governess, who failed to keep him in hand. He was always an avid reader of such books as came his way; and he received tutoring in Latin from a clerical uncle, so that he was eventually pronounced ready for school. The education act which was to provide state schooling for the children of Great Britain and Ireland lay far in the future. In any case, it behooved a gentleman's son to attend a gentleman's school, even if a cheap one. Accordingly young Shaw found himself in a place where teaching methods reflected the quality of ill-paid assistants. Small portions of Latin were handed out to be learned by rote, with a caning to follow if work was unsatisfactory. No boy learned anything of permanent value or burdened his memory for a moment longer than he could help with these boring assignments. After about a year, Sonny was discovered to have forgotten all he had learned from the clerical uncle.

It was Lee who insisted on a change, but his bohemian world of music had not fitted him to understand Dublin social distinctions. The school he fixed upon, though far better in theory and practice, was established largely for the sons of Catholic tradesmen. The humiliation for young Shaw was terrible. None of his old friends would play with him now. He for his part would not speak to his new associates, and at recreation he tagged miserably around the playground with the masters. But such was the power of Lee in that strange household that it was many months before the boy could prevail on his parents to make another transfer. His third school undoubtedly suited him best, yet as an example of its methods he recalled the history class in which each boy in alphabetical order was required to expound a few lines of the textbook assignment. So cut-and-dried was the arrangement that Shaw used to mark his lines in advance and read them quickly as he was filing into the classroom, never bothering his head about the rest of the daily portion.

Small wonder Shaw insisted that his early education had been gained in spite of school and that he was lucky the experience was over in five years. Like his mother, he had learned to retreat from a dull world; but being less musical than she, had turned to books. He learned English history from the plays of Shakespeare, European from the novels of Dumas. Dickens taught him about the nineteenth-century world, and Bunyan gave him the grand conception of allegory, in which problems are dramatized as people. Eager for experience in every kind of art, he penetrated the Dublin picture gallery to spend hours poring over the works of masters until the styles of individuals or schools of painting were familiar. Of course he knew by heart many works of musical masters and could whistle whole operas from beginning to end.

At sixteen, George Bernard Shaw was a curious mixture of unsophistication, indiscipline, ignorance, and wide artistic culture. Impatient to get out of school, he had no

Shaw (seated) at twenty years of age. A Dublin photograph taken with his friend Edward McNulty.

idea what he wanted to do. He had vague notions of being an artist, but could not draw. Musically he was thrown into the shade by his mother and sister. He had broken down discipline at school by making up stories, and he had used his boastful tongue and imagination more effectively than fists in self-defense. But, "You can't want a thing and have it too," he explained later. It had not occurred to him to wish to write because the ability to do so came as naturally to him as breathing, and he thought as little of it.

Anxious though he was to have done with education, his parents were if anything more eager than he. They needed money so badly that they already thought of getting him into a job at thirteen; but this arrangement fell through. Two years later, the Shaws' situation was more desperate than ever. Lee had published a book on his voice-training system in 1869 which had had a moderate success. Emboldened by its reception, he planned to go to London and make his fortune. This naturally involved the sale of the joint house and also of the cottage, which the Shaws had never owned. George Carr's business was limping along in its usual state of depression. The son already knew as much as the father had ever learned. Why continue his schooling when there could be no question of college or a profession?

George Carr Shaw might not be acceptable to his kindred in a social way, but he had enough influence to get his son a decent job. George Bernard was taken on in the estate office of Uniacke Townsend, one of the foremost in Dublin, handling the affairs of minors, absentee landlords, or others who needed expert advice on estate problems. No doubt the boy was told that his fortunes would be made if he worked steadily. He was lucky to have found good employment in what was after all a decent profession. Congratulations ignored the fact that there were other young gentlemen taken into the office, a few years older, with more education, and paying a premium. These were the real apprentices, and they were called "Mr." George Bernard was simply "Shaw." He filled the inkwells, changed the blotting paper, and was in fact, if not in theory, a simple office boy. His remuneration was eighteen shillings a month, hardly more than was earned by his mother's illiterate maids, who were housed in addition. Obviously, if he wanted to rise, he would have a long way to climb.

Meanwhile, Lucinda Elizabeth was preparing to break up her home. Lee's departure had robbed her life in Dublin of all purpose, and it is possible that she did not see how the family could live without him. Lucy, who was thought to be due for a brilliant singing career, needed better training. Meanwhile Agnes, in the carelessness of that ill-managed household, had caught tuberculosis from a housemaid. She was really ill, and the damp climate of Dublin was bad for her complaint. Lucinda Elizabeth did not see why she should not make money in London by helping Lee or perhaps preparing pupils before they entered the studio of the master.

Her husband was wax in her hands. He had lately fallen down in some sort of fit and had been frightened by the doctor into giving up alcohol. This unexpected change came twenty-five years too late. Lucinda Elizabeth, though in general kindly, was of all women the most unforgiving. She had condemned her husband long ago, and no consideration for his welfare could now move her. She sold the house and took the money. She established her two menfolk in a boardinghouse and left for London with her daughters. Nor did she bother to write often, though her husband manfully sent her a pound a week, which was all he could manage.

The change was hard on George Carr Shaw, whose disposition had grown more melancholy with temperance. There was nothing much for him to do in the long evenings but pore unhappily over accounts, getting occasional help from the son who was doing so well at his office. As for Bernard Shaw, his life was more exciting than it had been at home or at school, and tenderness and family feeling were unknown to him. He missed the music, but hardly felt lonely. He was acquiring some elementary social polish from the other apprentices with their college backgrounds and worldly wisdom. He held his own because of his knowledge of music, his love of an argument, and his glib tongue. Once Uniacke Townsend found him conducting an opera rehearsal in the office. On another occasion, he had to call him in and point out that the office was not a suitable place for arguments on religion. But he did not underestimate the boy's attention to his duties. The fact is, Townsend's office taught young Shaw the meaning of work. Ambitious, jealous of the privileged young men, and offered work that made sense, he soon proved his worth. When the cashier was detected in petty defalcations, young Shaw was temporarily given the job. He was soon confirmed in it at an increase in salary, a bargain for Townsend, who paid him less than an experienced man. The boy felt rich enough to clothe himself in top hat, tailcoat, and dark trousers like the older men in the office.

His relations with Townsend's young men were confined to office hours, but he soon began to make other friends. He formed an intimacy with a bank clerk called McNulty, who also had abilities above his present station. They discussed things together and wrote voluminous letters, working out their discontents and giving coherence to their developing thoughts. Both of them were dissatisfied with office life. The novelty had soon worn off for Shaw, and so had the pride in being cashier. Looked at more calmly, a good deal of what he did was distasteful. For instance, he had to collect slum rents for one of the clients of the firm. Even more of his job was simply dull. His prospects, which had appeared so bright, lost glamor as he understood the workings of the office. After holding the cashier's job for over a year, Shaw was suddenly demoted in favor of an untrained relative of the proprietor, who was getting experience with a view to quick advancement.

This insult to his pride caused Shaw's resignation after four years in Townsend's office. The firm, which thought well of him, offered another raise to keep him; but he would go. The fact was, he had only stayed so long because it was easier to know what he did not want than what he did. He was not quite twenty, and his inexperience was great. Only gradually had he learned to know himself. One of his office friends had remarked in his hearing that every youth thought he was bound to become a great man. With a sense of shock, young Shaw realized that without any thought on the subject, he had taken his future greatness for granted. Uncomfortably aware at last of his ambition, ought he not to do something about it?

No one could become great in Dublin. The town was too petty a place. Over the water lay London, center of a culture in which Dublin was a small provincial city. He would go to his mother, and he would not waste his time in an office again. Shaw packed his spare clothes, invested part of his savings in a one-way ticket to England, and turned his back on his past without regret. He did not revisit the land of his birth for thirty years.

1876–1885

Stranger in London

A TALL, young man with a pale face and light blue eyes, framed by conspicuous ears and orange hair neatly parted in the middle, stepped off a train in Euston station in the spring of 1876, carrying a carpetbag which contained his worldly possessions. As soon as he opened his mouth to ask for a cab, his accent proclaimed him a stranger to London. He was driven to his mother's house, where his welcome was not enthusiastic. Lucinda Elizabeth, though her courage had never faltered, had not found her new life easy. Instead of setting up the sort of studio he had conducted in Dublin, Lee had descended to charlatan tricks, promising wealthy mamas to turn out their daughters as accomplished singers after a course of twelve lessons. Lucinda Elizabeth, trained by his old thorough methods, was disgusted. She did not quarrel with Lee and was for a while seen at his studio. But in her own calm fashion she turned her back on the teacher who had dominated her life and started out to find her own pupils. Never did she show any sign of regret or affection for her master. When some years later Lee was found dead in his lodging, Lucinda Elizabeth heard the news unmoved, as though he had always been a stranger to her.

Her indifference was typical of her, but it may be also that she blamed Lee for not helping her more during those early years. While her son had been doing so well in Townsend's office, Lucinda Elizabeth had been toiling to support herself and her two daughters, the ailing Agnes in the Isle of Wight, and Lucy wherever she was most needed. Besides her husband's pound a week, Lucinda had some forty pounds a year of her own. There was in addition a legacy of four thousand pounds from her pawnbroker grandfather which was secured to her children, but which they released to her control as they became twenty-one. With this and her meager earnings she had managed, but her life had been hard. Poor Agnes had faded away and died, and it was now seen that Lucinda actually did miss the daughter to whom she had shown so little tenderness. She was consoling herself with a Ouija board in an attempt to penetrate beyond the grave.

Lucinda's establishment, an ugly house in a cheap district, was no more attractive or better kept than her Dublin homes had been. Its atmosphere was equally cold. So the boy had thrown up his job for no good reason! Probably he was only too like his father and would never come to good. Lucinda Elizabeth shrugged indifferent shoulders. George would have to find something to do, but meanwhile naturally he could have a bed at his mother's. There was plenty of room.

None of this particularly damped the young man's enthusiasm. He hardly would have known what to do

with a really warm welcome, whereas an endless struggle
with debt was a commonplace to him. But although Lucinda Elizabeth soon accepted the fact that her son would
be a burden around her neck for the rest of her life, Lucy
was by no means so resigned.

Lucy Carr Shaw, now approaching her middle twenties, was still polishing the perfection of her voice, pre-
liminary to starting on an operatic career. Lucy sang at
private parties and found occupation as soloist for amateur choirs; but, speaking broadly, she did not yet earn.
This state of affairs seemed natural to her because her
talents were sure in the end to bring fame and fortune.
Besides, in the respectable, middle-class world for which
Lucy secretly longed, unmarried daughters stayed at
home. On the other hand, when her brother, who had
been so decently settled in life, turned up in London
without a job, Lucy felt disgraced. She had a sharp
tongue, and she poured out the reproaches from which
Lucinda Elizabeth refrained.

Her brother's obstinacy was equal to Lucy's. At first, to
be sure, he still had a little money. A short while later he
turned twenty-one and relinquished his share of the family inheritance to his mother. He felt a right to claim some
time for looking around.

He began to explore London widely on foot and soon
discovered the National Gallery, where he continued the
art studies which he had started in Dublin. Later he penetrated to the reading room of the British Museum, that
free research center where, amid other eccentrics, Karl
Marx could still be seen scowling angrily over piles of

books and papers. At home he drove his mother to distraction by picking out operas of Wagner on the piano. Wagner's operas were far too modern for Lucinda Elizabeth's taste. Her son's delight in them was almost a greater trial to her nerves than his idleness.

Such occupations led nowhere, but as a more practical measure young Shaw turned to Lee, disregarding the break which had occurred with his mother and sister. He helped by playing accompaniments at musical parties and in return was asked to ghost-write musical criticism for Lee, whose talents did not include ability in writing. Unluckily the forthright criticisms of the young reviewer offended managers, who withdrew their advertisements. The paper went out of business, and Shaw lost the payments which he had been splitting with Lee, as well, presumably, as free tickets to musical affairs. He had gained a few introductions, however; and his family had some connections in London. Every so often a well-meaning person recommended him for a job which it taxed his quick wits to escape. He personally preferred to try his luck with free-lance articles, which were rejected by every paper in London. In the course of his first nine years, he made five pounds by this means out of one short article, one advertisement for a patent medicine, and one set of verses commissioned by an acquaintance.

Three years actually passed in this fashion. It must be remembered that the boy had little formal education and no social experience. He had his ambition to make a name in the world, but he had few contacts with people who could show him how to do so. He was invited to call by a gregarious artist named Cecil Lawson, whose parties were well known among the artistic set. Very sensibly he had fortified himself by studying a book on etiquette in the reading room of the British Museum. Lucinda Elizabeth, who never dined out and hardly bothered to serve a family meal, had left her children to learn the niceties of party manners by instinct if at all. Unluckily, in the social sphere a little practice is worth a great deal of theory. Shy by nature and conscious of his deficiencies, Shaw more than once spent twenty minutes pacing the street outside Lawson's door before he could summon up courage to ring the bell. When he did get inside, he was aware that he talked too much and contradicted too often in order to cover up his inner panic. But he made himself go again and again, ashamed to harbor great ambitions if he were content to be a social coward. Presently Lawson died, and Shaw's education in the ways of the world declined once more.

By 1879, things were so bad in the household that he could no longer resist the family pressure. Through the efforts of a cousin, Shaw found a job with the Edison Telephone Company. It consisted in persuading people to allow telephone wires to be installed across their premises. As a position, it had little future; and it was unfitted by its very nature for a shy man. Shaw held it, however, for about six months until Edison's company was absorbed by Bell's. The new organization was anxious to keep its employee, who had demonstrated the same efficiency and willingness to work he had shown at Townsend's. But experience had merely convinced him that it was mad-ness to waste his time in uncongenial employment. He refused the company's offer and was penniless again.

By this time he had gained a sense of purpose. He knew what he was going to do, namely, to write novels. Accordingly, in 1879 he bought sixpence-worth of white paper, folded it in quarters, and started to cover it in a small, neat hand. Once more it was obvious that the young man was not really lazy. Indeed his system may seem to show more industry than inspiration. He set himself to fill five pages a day, keeping so rigidly to schedule that he would break off in the middle of a sentence when his task was completed. On the other hand, if he missed a day, he wrote ten pages on the next to make it up. *Immaturity* was finished before the end of the year and subsequently rejected by every publisher in London. While the author was finding it hard to lay his hands on an occasional sixpence to dispatch it in some new direction, he was busily at work on a second novel, then a third, a fourth, a fifth, all of which eventually joined *Immaturity* on its rounds without result.

Their lack of success is understandable. They were not like other books, and they did not read easily because plot meant less to their author than ideas. For character he showed a certain gift; yet writing for London, the young man from Dublin did not really know his world. His sense of humor peeps through only here and there, so that situations which in his later work would have been richly comic merely seem peculiar and unexpected. The real importance of these five novels to Shaw lies not in their value. They were the exercises which taught him to write. For over five years he was regularly trying to express ideas in an artistic form, never allowing disinclination, fatigue, or disappointment to put him off.

The failure of so much effort was the harder because his necessities were great. That respectable tailcoat which he had bought for Townsend's was now green with age. Its cuffs grew ragged and were trimmed with scissors. Only its tails concealed two holes in the seat of his trousers. The brim of his top hat was so limp that he had to wear it back to front in order to be able to raise it to a chance acquaintance. His boots were in holes, the uppers cracked and broken. He could hardly have got a job if he wanted one now. Only in the evenings was he respectable, for gentlemen then wore evening dress to every function after dark, and luckily artificial light conceals much wear.

He was not embittered by his hard experience, and he never gave way to despair. But he did become more solitary as he grew less presentable, and he began to adopt eccentric ways. In 1882, for instance, he decided to become a vegetarian, convinced by Shelley that animals are our brothers and we should not eat them. Actually this gave him a pretext for avoiding his mother's atrocious stews by dining, when he could muster up the cash, in cheap vegetarian restaurants. If he could not, the servant might bring him a poached egg, half-cold and swimming with water, or he would even stay his hunger with brown bread and apples. Luckily his appetite was small. Long ago he had decided that the Shaw family, in the persons of his father and uncles, had consumed their fair share of alcohol for his generation as well as their own. Tea and coffee he would not touch, as being stimulants also. His spirits needed little but company and conversation to set them soaring.

In 1882, he caught smallpox during an epidemic, in spite of having been given a vaccination. The experience left him with a lifelong hatred for vaccination which persisted in spite of every evidence of its value. His whole relationship towards doctors was an odd one. He used them if he was really ill, but this did not happen often. In general, he suspected them of pretending to know much more than they did, and was full of fancies about the best way to preserve his health and avoid their assistance.

In 1885 George Carr Shaw died in Dublin, not greatly lamented by his family, who could not have afforded to go to the funeral, even if such a notion had entered their heads. In the last thirteen years he had only once paid a week's visit to Lucinda Elizabeth, while she had never again set foot in Ireland. Surprisingly enough, he left a small life insurance, which was duly paid into Lucinda Elizabeth's hands. The consequence was a notation in Shaw's diary for April of the year: "Ordered clothes at Jaeger's — the first new garments I have had for years. These will be paid out of the insurance on my father's life." They consisted of a suit with unlined coat, vest and pants, collars and tie, all woolen.

It would be delightful to think that Shaw looked less peculiar at last, but such was probably not the case. Jaeger's was a store with a mission, dedicated to the theories of a Prussian zoologist called Gustav Jaeger, whose notion was that human beings should be clothed exclusively in animal fibers such as wool and camelhair. With the exuberance of a crank, he promised freedom from the common cold, rheumatism, and a long list of other ills to people who were wise enough to avoid silk, linen, and cotton — for synthetic fabrics had not yet been heard of. The idea became the rage among health faddists; and when Shaw could afford them, his sheets, shirts, underwear, and even handkerchiefs became all woolen.

Unluckily Jaeger developed theories on the design of clothes as well as their structure, and Shaw in these early years was obstinate in trying what he believed conducive to health. One friend a few years later describes a suit of his as "a single garment or combination in brown knitted wool complete from sleeves to ankle in one piece." Another complains of a Jaeger suit which shrank in the rain and stiffened up until it rattled in a manner irritating beyond bearing.

Shaw had started to grow a beard when he had smallpox, not because his face was scarred, but very probably because for a while he could not shave. It grew in very sparsely and hardly added to the distinction of his appearance. By persevering, however, he finally achieved a full beard and moustache. In photographs this looks rather well, appearing to balance the curious effect of one bushy eyebrow raised high, the other depressed as though he were winking. Those who knew him at this time, however, did not admire it. In contrast to his white face and pale eyes, said someone or other, his carroty hair and beard gave him the impression of an unskillfully poached

egg. He was matchstick thin, and his big nose was red.
His ears stuck out like handles. The best one could say
was that when he started to talk, one forgot his appearance . . . "if he can ever be said to begin," his friend
added, "for he talks always, in his fine Irish brogue."

Shabby he might be, eccentric, obscure, and self-suffi-
cient; but he was not tongue-tied. He was bursting with
nervous energy for which his trade of novel-writing gave
no outlet. Eagerly he joined a debating club called the
Zetetical Society, or in plain English the Seekers. Here

Shaw in a double-breasted woolen suit from Jaeger's.

atheism and evolution were discussed or Mill's principle that the greatest good of the greatest number is the true guide to moral conduct; and here in the course of a debate Shaw rose to speak in public for the first time in his life. It was a dreadful occasion. He was shaking with nerves and could not read his notes, much less remember them. He sat down miserably certain that he had made a fool of himself. There and then he made a resolution that he would attend every meeting and speak every time until he had conquered his shyness. The third time he appeared, he had already made such an impression that he was asked to take the chair. He did so as though the action were commonplace; but when the secretary asked him to sign the minutes at the end of the meeting, his hand was shaking so badly that he could hardly trace his signature.

Presently he began to branch out. There were always dozens of debates and lectures in London, entrance to which was free. Literary societies, societies for vegetarians, freethinkers, and would-be reformers of every sort popped up like mushrooms. He joined them and started to ask questions "exasperating enough to make a worm turn or a rabbit fight." A record in the minutes of the Browning Society gives an example of his technique. A certain Mr. Oldham, Shaw complains, "spoke of Browning as a great poet who preferred not to express himself clearly, and seemed to have a notion that Browning thought out a thing quite clearly, and then immediately sat down and thought how he could make it unintelligible and prevent anybody from reading it. That would reduce Mr. Brown-

ing to a malignant demon who deliberately wished to confuse and puzzle the human race. In reference to all this
about Browning's obscurity, he (Shaw) wanted to know
to whom he was obscure. If it was to be laid down that a
poet must be plain to everybody, you came to Dr. Watts
at once." No doubt Mr. Oldham turned to bay, and people recognized that when that red-bearded fellow spoke
up, the debate crackled. Shaw found himself the best-
known man in the crank societies of London.

In 1882, pursuing this policy of learning how to speak,
he attended a lecture by Henry George, an early American socialist whose influence was to be great on Shaw's
generation in England. Hitherto Shaw had largely concerned himself with the conflict between religion and science. George's eloquence fixed his attention on economics, and he invested a precious sixpence in his *Progress
and Poverty*, which excited him tremendously. Brought
up on the fringes of capitalistic society, forced to struggle
for what came easily to other people, Shaw readily understood how an indictment of society had special meaning
for him. He had found a cause and was fit to be its cham-
pion.

After this experience, he turned his attention to people
of like mind. A new group called the Democratic Federation, founded by H. M. Hyndman, had recently been established on the principles of Marx, whose influence was
considerable in Europe, but whose person was quite unknown in London, despite his residence of more than
twenty years. At a meeting, therefore, Shaw appeared,
eagerly quoting from *Progress and Poverty*. The Dem-

ocratic Federation was not willing to put up with a rival prophet, and it disposed of George and Shaw in a single breath by remarking that no one was qualified to discuss such subjects until he had read Marx. Shaw immediately retired to the British Museum, where he was forced to wrestle with *Das Kapital* in a French version since, though written in England and published fifteen years before, it had not yet been translated into the language. One marvels at Shaw, whose French cannot have been good. He had his reward when he returned to the Democratic Federation in triumph, to discover that Hyndman was in fact the only other who had really read the book.

Das Kapital was a landmark in Shaw's life. Later on, when he understood more economics, he rejected a large part of its theory. But he was swept off his feet by the surge of Marx's anger against the greed and inhumanity of the nineteenth-century industrial system. *Das Kapital* showed him that the organization of society was wrong, and it gave him a hope of changing it to something better. It showed him the fundamental importance of economics. It made him a political agitator and a man with a cause which soon expressed itself in his last two novels as well as in his speeches. The arduous training through which he had put himself was justified when he had found a purpose.

1885–1894
The Exciting Years

In the British Museum one day in the early eighties a journalist and budding dramatic critic called William Archer was aware of a young man of startling appearance who was reading Karl Marx in French, sandwiched at intervals by the orchestral score of Wagner's *Tristan und Isolde*. The combination intrigued him, and he made up his mind to make the acquaintance. The friendship which ensued was lifelong. In manner and appearance Archer was rigidly conventional. As a critic, he was often unfavorable to Shaw's dramas. Notwithstanding, there was more in him than generally appeared. He had his share of sensibility, and even of humor, though he concealed it from the casual eye. Nor were his artistic judgments really old-fashioned. He was an enthusiast for the new drama, notably for Ibsen, whose works were more or less unknown in London.

Along such lines the two had much to talk of. Archer, who had influence where Shaw did not, soon became busy exerting it in his friend's favor. In 1885, therefore, thanks to Archer's efforts, Shaw actually began to get jobs. He reviewed books for *The Pall Mall Gazette* and was appointed art critic to *The World*. Neither of these paid much, but his first year's income doubled what the family had lost by the death of his father. As an art critic, to be sure, he was only fair. His interest was in subject rather than technique, but at least his copy was entertaining. This perhaps was just as well, since he was never willing to have his stuff cut about or rewritten according to the whims of editors. He was difficult, sometimes impossible to deal with; but people put up with him because his capacity for saying outrageous things with an air was already developed. "During the past month Art has suffered an unusually severe blow at the hands of the Royal Academy by the opening of the annual exhibition at Burlington House." The readers of *The World* sat up and took notice.

Shaw was getting to his feet at last, thanks mainly to Archer. Meanwhile, however, more important things had come into his life than money. He had discovered a mission, a kindred spirit, and a group poised for the right sort of action.

The Fabian Society was founded in 1884 as an offshoot of a vague group called the Fellowship of the New Life, which had been started by an Anglo-American philosopher of Scottish origin named Thomas Davidson. The general idea of the Fellowship had been to live the higher life as an example to other people, and an ideal community in Brazil had been suggested. This drastic proposal brought about a division. Besides those who believed in regeneration by spiritual means, there were others who thought the crux of the modern problem was economic. Such men were skeptical about ideal communities and added that the proper field for their endeavors was England. Out of this dispute the Fabian Society was born, taking its title and motto from a story invented for the purpose by one of its members. Fabius, the Roman General who defeated Hannibal by guerrilla tactics, was said to have advised his fellows to avoid direct action until the right moment, and then to strike hard. Following the first part of this advice, the Fabians announced themselves as socialists who rejected a violent revolution in favor of peaceful permeation and propaganda.

The first proceeding of the Fabian Society was to put out a little pamphlet entitled "Why Are the Many Poor?" which fell very naturally into the hands of Shaw. He took notice of its cautious tone and classical name. In Hyndman's working-class movement he felt a fish out of water. The intellectual pretensions of the Fabians might suit him better. He turned up in May of 1884 to find a collection of well-meaning cranks, some prominently connected with psychical research, yet all concerned, as he was, with tackling their problems in an intelligent manner. Luckily he already knew the man who could give them direction.

It was in the Zetetical Society that Shaw had first set eyes on Sidney Webb, whose mere appearance cannot have impressed him. Webb was unusually short and delicately made with tiny hands and feet. In contrast, his head looked disproportionately massive. His face was vast and oval, his nose hooked, his forehead high, and his eyes bulging. A small chin-beard gave the whole a fin-

icking impression, while adding further to its size. No
one ever had less of a presence than Sidney Webb, though
his kindliness and unselfconscious manners disarmed
critics. What attracted Shaw about him was his knowledge.

> He knew all about the subject of debate; knew
> more than the lecturer; knew more than anybody
> present; had read everything that had ever been
> written on the subject; and remembered all the
> facts that bore on it. He used notes, ticked them
> off one by one, threw them away, and finished
> with a coolness and clearness that to me, in my
> then trembling state, seemed miraculous. This
> young man was the ablest man in England.

It was not an unreasonable verdict. Webb's abilities
were indeed extraordinary. He could read a page at a
glance and remember everything on it. His mind was a
complete index-card file wherein all information which
had ever entered it was instantly ready for use on any occasion. He was never idle and never bored, so that the
accumulation of useful facts went on within him daily. At
the time Shaw met him, he was a clerk in the Colonial Office, having risen to that position from fairly humble beginnings by the simple process of being first in every
examination he entered. His father was a Cockney tax-
collector, while his mother, uneasy in the presence of Sidney's gentlemen friends, addressed them as "Sir."

Webb, too, had heard Henry George and had been
turning in the direction of socialism. Presently he and
Shaw, so strangely contrasted in appearance and intel-

Shaw at about thirty, a photograph of the 1880's.

lectual gifts, were inseparable. They complimented each other, Shaw providing the humor, imagination, and dash, while Sidney rolled up an argument or managed a meeting with consummate address. The Fabian Society, in acquiring such recruits, was quite transformed. Power fell into their hands because of their abilities and because they stood together without the slightest shadow ever falling on their relationship. Webb brought into the society Sydney Olivier, another Colonial Office clerk, and Graham Wallas, a college friend of his. The four young men began to live their lives in common. The Colonial Office did not open till eleven in the morning so that there was plenty of time for informal consultations or a share in Shaw's breakfast of brown bread and cocoa. Lucinda Elizabeth did not care for socialists, whom she thought ungentlemanly. In particular she was not impressed by Sidney Webb whom she dismissed succinctly as "eating greedily, talking speedily, and looking weedily." Meanwhile, the Colonial Office found things growing lively as a red-bearded young man dropped in with urgent problems which had nothing to do with colonies, and the records of the Fabian Society were kept in a desk drawer.

When evening came, there was plenty going on. The young men involved themselves in a serious study of economics, walking clear out to Hampstead, rain or shine, every two weeks for a meeting in which they read long papers and argued out theories. Shaw put himself out on these walks to dazzle the others, while from the heights of their university educations they criticized his logic. In the Fabian Society itself, the application of a serious mind like Webb's to the problem of making England a socialist state gave impetus to a great deal of detailed study which was new to the whole movement. In the

early days when Shaw had been asked how long it would
take to set up the socialist state, come the revolution, he
had thought he was cautious in answering, "a fortnight."
Later, the Fabians formed a parliamentary group in
which each member was minister of a department and
had the duty of drawing up proper bills and getting them
through committee. The complications of these practical
processes were a revelation.

Meanwhile, the primary function of the Fabian Society
was not self-education. Its members took an active part in
propaganda, not merely on their own behalf, but for the
benefit of the regular socialist societies, such as Hyndman's. Every Sunday, sometimes two or three times, and
a number of weekdays, Shaw would be off to speak in
clubs, on street corners, in little halls and cellars, even in
churches, in every place where men wanted unpaid speakers. By refusing anything but his fare, he preserved the
right to speak on what he pleased, working out lectures
on subjects he wanted to understand, such as rent, profit,
wages, cooperation, trade-unionism, or democracy. Every
so often he became involved in curious adventures. One
day, for instance, he found himself in a small, shabby
room talking to anarchists, "twenty enthusiasts for de-
stroying all authority." They were very mild men, he remarks, and not really dangerous — all except one man, "a
fragile and mild creature, and he really was dangerous,
and he had provided himself with a dynamite bomb, on
which he was sitting during the entire time I was addressing that meeting — a fact which I was not aware of at the
time, or perhaps I should not have addressed them with

so much self-assurance as I did." Shortly afterwards the mild man took his bomb into the park and, apparently by accident while fiddling with it, blew himself up.

On another occasion Shaw was assigned to address an outdoor meeting; but it rained so hard that nobody turned up except the police who had been posted to keep order. Shaw cast his eye on those policemen preparing to listen just long enough to be sure that he was not preaching sedition or inciting to riot. He vowed he would make them hang on his words for an hour, and he spoke to them with such fire and passion that ever afterwards he could close his eyes and summon up a picture of the rain and their dripping capes and the empty park.

It was all such glorious fun! How they laughed together! What arguments they all had, and how much work they got through! But though this was living, it was not livelihood. All of the others were better off than Shaw, although he was giving more unpaid time than any of them. Luckily someone else appeared to the rescue.

Mrs. Annie Besant was at this time the most famous, or at least the most notorious, woman in London. Marrying too young to know her own mind, she had parted from her husband because she developed religious doubts which he would neither answer nor tolerate. By chance in the course of her controversy with him, she discovered a great gift of eloquence. As a result, she speedily became a public figure, working closely with Charles Bradlaugh, an atheist and radical member of Parliament. Together the two were arrested on criminal charges for publishing a book on birth control. Acquitted after a sensational trial, she was then sued by her husband for recovery of their daughter, on the grounds that she was not fit to bring up her child. Frank Besant won his case and branded his wife, whom he refused to divorce.

All radical circles impinged on one another, so that Shaw's reputation as a speaker was soon contrasted with the very different gifts of Mrs. Besant. She accepted the implicit challenge and attended a meeting of his with the

The early Fabians at work together.
L to R: Shaw, Beatrice and Sidney Webb, Graham Wallas.

express intention of demolishing him. But when she did get up to speak, to the astonishment of all she proved to have been converted. She joined the Fabian Society and was soon seen everywhere on the same platforms as Shaw. Annie Besant was a young and beautiful woman still. Shaw's Dublin days had taught him a courtly gallantry, especially pleasing to ladies who had no experience of Irish manners. He escorted Annie home and went in with her to play duets on the piano.

Annie Besant was editor of a magazine called *Our Corner*, and she saw a chance to help Shaw out by publishing his novels in serial form. *Our Corner*, however, had not been founded by socialists, so that its supporters fell away as Annie's involvement with the Fabian Society increased. Eventually it was so nearly bankrupt that she was reduced to paying Shaw secretly out of her own pocket. Discovering this, he refused to accept any more money. His relations with Annie, despite his gratitude as an author, were growing uneasy. For she was more in love than he and was making demands.

With the exuberance of youth, the Fabian Society flung itself into the battles of the labor movement. 1886 was a year of trade depression, and many a man who had been laid off was facing starvation. There was more working-class agitation in England than there had been in forty years. Windows were broken in Pall Mall. Mass meetings grew bigger and more threatening all year long. By 1887, the authorities were growing anxious. The moment they attempted to preserve order, the socialists raised a cry for free speech and rallied the workers. The crisis came on November 13, when a great mass meeting was announced for Trafalgar Square. The police refused a permit, but the workers ignored this.

Two contingents assembled to make the march through London, the northern one gathering on Clerkenwell Green, where they listened to the exhortations of Shaw and the fiery eloquence of Annie Besant.

The pair set out together, marching modestly in the midst of the procession. Thus when the head of the procession came in sight of Trafalgar Square and the police charged it with bludgeons, neither Annie nor Shaw was overrun. She looked at him, though; and he felt a fool. Quite plainly he ought to give some heroic sign of leadership, but what? He said to Annie, "You must keep out of this."

With that he walked forward and saw the end of the conflict. Everybody was scattering now, and the police were retreating. It was easy for individuals to get into the square. He did so, but there was nothing to be done. The soldiers had been called out; and cavalry were already in possession, riding around and forcing everybody on foot to keep walking. Annie Besant, who had tried to get there by a back way, did not appear.

The fiasco of "Bloody Sunday" taught Shaw a rough and ready lesson about the ineffectiveness of mobs which he never forgot. At a great protest meeting, Annie Besant called for another march; but he demolished her by pointing out that revolution meant not police with bludgeons but soldiers with machine guns. He had discovered for himself that the people were incompetent to run their own affairs. In a year or so when unemployment decreased again and agitation died away, he realized also that they could be cheaply bribed to be quiet.

The proper business of the Fabians was not promoting "Bloody Sundays." In later years Shaw always maintained that at the first sign of revolution, he should take refuge under his bed, emerging only when the shooting had died down, to organize the future. The Fabian Society had erred through inexperience. It did not do so again. Its next important work was the production of *Fabian Essays*, edited by Shaw and containing contributions from Sidney Webb, Annie Besant and the others. This unassuming little volume, sold out its first edition at once, has sold more or less ever since, and still is a classic. In it, the Fabians began to educate their public.

1886–1895

Women and Dramatics

"My!" exclaimed Sidney Webb in mild astonishment, "you do warm both hands before the fire of life!"

He was not commenting on the restless energy of his friend, but on his ability to carry on flirtations with as many as six ladies at once. Being Sidney Webb, he took for granted that none of these diversions would ever make Shaw late for a meeting or interfere with his Fabian work. But the fact that they did not is really remarkable when one considers that several of the ladies were not connected with the Fabians. How Shaw found time for them, nobody knows, since they never came first.

For the greater part of his first nine years in London, Shaw made no approach to a woman. He had nothing decent to wear and could hardly have afforded the price of a cup of coffee or a bus fare. Marriage, since he could not support himself, was not to be thought of. Monastic though his life was, however, he dreamed about women — saw one in the British Museum and wrote her into a novel. He needed an emotional give-and-take for his creative work. His instinct was to place himself on familiar terms with a woman, to woo her with extravagant compliments, to tell her he adored her, and to enjoy the relationship, rather than the person. It never occurred to him to count the world well lost for anybody, and he says himself about marriage: "The greatest sacrifice in marriage is the sacrifice of the adventurous attitude towards life: the being settled. Those who are born tired may crave for settlement; but to fresher and stronger spirits it is a form of suicide."

His first love was a girl called Alice Lockett, by profession a nurse and a singing pupil of his mother's. Alice, a nice girl of no remarkable gifts, was wooed by extravagant words and flattered by long letters until she scarcely knew what she herself wanted. Shaw clearly had no thought of marriage; but when she repulsed his familiarities, he sent her pages and pages in his fine, neat hand, drawing a distinction between that horrid prude, Miss Lockett, and his Alice, so good, so sweet, so fair. Her heart was melted, and yet she could not but wonder if his was touched at all. He was like quicksilver in her hand, which might at any minute run out through her fingers if she tried to clasp it. And how brightly he glittered! How incessantly the soft Irish brogue went on and on. If there was any heartache in this affair, it surely was Miss Lockett's. And did she understand the half of what he said?

Jenny Patterson, who followed next, was more tenacious. She also was a pupil of Lucinda Elizabeth, a youngish widow with modest means, good-looking, dark, and passionate. What Jenny wanted, she was bound to have. In effect, Jenny held the quicksilver for a year or

two. Eventually, however, her lover met Florence Farr
and admired her for her tolerance and good humor, qualities which Jenny conspicuously did not possess. Jenny in
a rage was a perfect fury. Her jealousy caused her to make
terrible scenes which Shaw endured because he was too
kindhearted to be indifferent when she was unhappy.
When she actually pursued the pair to Florence's lodging and tried to attack her rival, his patience was exhausted. She bombarded him with letters and telegrams
for months afterwards, but he never answered.

Meanwhile, Annie Besant, who was not free to marry
him legally, had drawn up a form of association between
them which she wanted him to sign. Had she but known
it, this was the surest way of getting rid of him. Annie
had too much dignity to make scenes; but her hair turned
gray and she began to look haggard when Shaw no longer
dropped in to play duets. She gave up the Fabians. May
Morris, daughter of a famous artist and socialist, married someone else, apparently in a fit of independence.
The pair made the mistake of inviting Shaw to stay with
them for a longish convalescence. He came, and his devastating charm did its work. He was too honorable to
have an intrigue with the wife of a friend, so he de-
parted. Immediately May Morris left her husband and
did not return. Edith Nesbitt, wife of yet another col-
league, openly pursued him; but he fended her off.

Such preoccupations and a frantic round of Fabian activities did not prevent him from making his mark as a
critic at last. In 1888, he became music critic of *The Star*
and commenced a famous series of articles over the signa-

ture of "Corno di Bassetto" or Basset Horn, which continued for six years. The general British public now discovered to its surprise and joy that writing on music could be fun. Conventional musicians, meantime, could not deny that "Corno di Bassetto's" knowledge of music was thorough; though they did deplore his expressing his personal prejudices. What else, queried "Corno di Bassetto" unashamed, was a critic for? He did not scruple to dismiss the Polish pianist Paderewski with: "His touch, light or heavy, is the touch that hurts; and the glory of his playing is the glory that attends murder on a large scale when impetuously done." Nor did he ever refrain from introducing his own personality into his articles, telling his readers: "There is nothing that soothes me more after a long and maddening course of pianoforte recitals than to sit and have my teeth drilled by a finely skilled hand."

Outworn conventions of the opera stage became objects of his special ridicule; and he advised the Philharmonic Society to retire its directors at the age of ninety-five so as to be more up-to-date. He spared nobody, writing of his sister Lucy, who had the leading role in a popular light opera, that she sang "without the slightest effort and without the slightest point." Laying about him, he remarked that "there are some sacrifices which should not be demanded twice from any man; and one of them is listening to Brahms' Requiem." In fact, he wrote in accordance with his own maxim: "In this world if you do not say a thing in an irritating way, you may just as well not say it at all, since nobody will trouble themselves about anything that does not trouble them."

He never forgot that he was writing for the musical public, not for musicians. To him, this public consisted of people who stood in a queue to pay for cheap seats which they could scarcely afford. For their sake, he remarked on music in unexpected places, complimenting the massed bands of the Salvation Army and the artistry of a street musician playing on the cornet. For their sake, he was careful to avoid musical jargon.

He had a regular income from this work, yet he was as ever impecunious. "I was to have had an advance of ten pounds for my expenses," he wrote to the treasurer of the Fabian Society as he started out to attend a distant meeting. "Eventually my mother advanced it . . . Funds being low, you had better let her have it back again in the course of this week, lest I find her an emaciated corpse on my return." As money came in, it was spent. He had not so far aspired to the luxury of a bank account.

Shaw was always going somewhere, either to a concert, to a meeting of the Fabian Executive Committee, or to make a speech. As he said later on, if you wanted to know him, you had to do what he did, since he never had time for social occasions. His articles, his speeches, even those eloquent letters in which he wooed various ladies were written in buses or trains or even scribbled on the coping of a wall under a street lamp, where inspiration had come upon him as he was striding home in the dark. He had taken to carrying little notebooks, which were easier to handle under these conditions than loose paper. He had even taught himself Pitman's shorthand, so as to waste no space and lose no time when he set ideas down.

Though he had given up trying to write novels, he was beginning his proper work at last.

In 1885, he and William Archer had long talks about the state of British drama. Archer was an admirer of Ibsen and had translated some of his work, though he had not so far been able to get it performed. Nobody in England was yet writing plays which dealt with anything except romance. Deploring this, the two young men would have liked to start a new trend. Archer, however, complained that though he knew all about constructing a plot, he had no notion of how to write dialogue. Shaw replied that dialogue flowed out of him with ease, but he never had a plot.

A collaboration was the obvious answer. Accordingly, Archer worked out a scenario which, by the rules of the game as it was then played, ought to have succeeded. Indeed, he was too cautious to make up a plot of his own; he merely adapted one which had been previously popular. Action started in a castle on the Rhine, for no reason except that this made a pretty scene in which to introduce a wealthy Englishman traveling with his daughter and niece. These two young ladies, the romantic and the comedy heroines, became entangled with a young man who appeared to propose to the daughter under the impression that she was the penniless niece. He was soon appalled to discover that the money with which he had allied himself came from the rents of slum property in London. Eventually the way was clear for a noble gesture and a great renunciation of the money.

Shaw listened to this plot, thanked his collaborator, and

for some six weeks never mentioned the matter. Archer, who saw him in the British Museum every day, perceived that he was covering pages in neat shorthand at the rate of about three words a minute. Imagining that this was some weighty treatise, he said nothing.

At the end of this time, Shaw accosted his friend. "Look here, I've finished the first act of that play of ours and haven't yet come to your plot. In fact, I've forgotten it. Do tell it to me once more."

Archer was not best pleased, but Shaw solemnly assured him that a play never begins until Act Two. Archer's annoyance, however, was greater three days after when Shaw spoke again.

"I've written three pages of the second act and have used up all your plot. Can you let me have some more to go on with?"

Archer pointed out that a plot was a constructed whole and that to ask more was like demanding extra arms and legs on a statue. Shaw tried to pacify him and offered to read the first two acts aloud when they were finished. He did so. Archer listened puzzled to the first act and fell asleep in the second. On awaking, he declared the collaboration was at an end. Shaw took his work to a well-known dramatist, who thought it lacking in incident and queried, "Where's your murder?" Writing plays, concluded the would-be author, was not his line. He tossed the manuscript aside. Seven years later an opportunity arose for him to use it.

J. T. Grein, a Dutch-born dramatic critic living in London, organized the production of some English plays in

Amsterdam in 1890. He used the money thus made to form a society in London for the production of plays which did not comply with the formulas demanded by actor-managers in the big theaters. He opened in 1891 with a performance of Ibsen's *Ghosts*, which is a study of the social effects of venereal disease. It was greeted with cries of horror in the public press, creating such a sensation that the English stage was never quite so unsophisticated thereafter.

About a year before, the Fabian Society, at a loss for a subject for a series of summer meetings, had been persuaded by Shaw to consider socialism in contemporary literature. The sensation of the series was Shaw's own lecture on Ibsen, which he shortly thereafter enlarged and published as a lengthy treatise. Accordingly, he was known to admirers of Ibsen, including Grein. In the course of a walk together, Shaw developed the theme that English drama was bursting to express itself in new ways, given the opportunity of production. Grein, however, after a long search was unable to discover a single example of native British drama in what was beginning to be called the modern style. Never one to be worsted in an argument, Shaw fished out his seven-year-old unfinished masterpiece, added a third act, and entitled it *Widowers' Houses*. Grein produced it on December 9, 1892.

Widowers' Houses had by now little to do with Archer's original plot, except that the opening took place at a castle on the Rhine. The hero and heroine became engaged without delay, and the problem of the play had nothing to do with love. The heroine's father was a wealthy man, whose income was derived from slum rents. But when the young man refused to accept such tainted money, he was rapidly shown that his own unearned income was derived from a mortgage on precisely the same property. What good would it do the slum dwellers if he renounced his money? If he invested it elsewhere at a lower rate, would it not acquire some fresh taint without his knowledge? Gradually the young man was drawn into being a willing partner in the older man's dubious schemes. He married the lady; but we cannot presume him to have lived happily ever after, since she was by no means the milk-and-water young miss of romantic drama. On the contrary, she was a sensuous, passionate girl whose furious temper came as a deliberate shock to sentimental dreamers.

It is difficult to imagine ourselves in the nineties when such a theme and such a heroine could cause an uproar. Shaw's socialist friends, who were strong in the audience, received the play with hearty cheers. Conventional playgoers responded with hisses. A tumult after the curtain fell was quelled by the author, who was well used to charming a hostile audience. He asked his hearers to discriminate between the actors, who had done their best, and himself, with whom the fault lay. Retiring amid cheers, he left the last word to the critics.

Next day in the morning papers the critics exploded, including William Archer, who told Shaw he knew nothing about his subject and had no understanding of a woman's nature. He advised him to give up spending

time and energy on "a form of production for which he
has no special ability." To this unkindest cut of all Shaw
replied on a postcard:

> Here am I who have collected slum rents
> weekly with these hands, and for 4½ years been
> behind the scenes of the middle-class landowner
> — who have philandered with women of all sorts
> and sizes — and I am told gravely to go to nature
> and give up apriorising about such matters by
> you, you sentimental Sweet Lavendery recluse.

Truth was, Shaw did not care what the critics said. The
abuse he had aroused was almost as violent as that poured
out on *Ghosts*. It had served to convince him that he was
a born dramatist. His time and energy were certainly going to be spent on this form of production.

His head was never to be turned by winning any sudden success. His next play, *The Philanderer*, about his
own amorous adventures and with himself in the leading
part, was rejected by Grein's Independent Theatre because the roles were too difficult for the cast. With the
best will in the world, the Independent Theatre could
only work with the actors available, all of whom were
trained in the old declamatory style and accustomed to
wringing pathos or romance out of every situation. *The
Philanderer*, which starts with the furious scene which
had actually happened when Jenny Patterson tried to attack Florence Farr, had no ideal women; and the loves
which it describes, though realistic, were never romantic.
What was worse, Shaw turned the play into a satire on
the modern woman, about whom a great deal had been

said and written since a recent sensational performance
of Ibsen's *A Doll's House*. In fact, the play offended
progressive friends and conservative enemies with an im-
partial hand. In particular Archer, whose devotion to Ibsen approached idolatry, was so angry that he would
hardly speak to Shaw when he ran across him.

This failure did not discourage Shaw. He was used to
it by now. His novels, serialized by Annie Besant or in
some other small magazine, had later achieved publication in book form. He remarks that in 1889 his royalty on
An Unsocial Socialist was two shillings and tenpence. It
had risen by 1891 to seven shillings and tenpence, nearly
trebling his take, as he gaily points out. He was perfectly
ready to go on writing unpopular plays, and a friend had
suggested to him a romantic story of the relationship between a mother and a daughter. In Shaw's hands this
turned in 1893 into *Mrs. Warren's Profession*. The mother
is a successful prostitute who has brought up her daughter in ignorance of what she does. The daughter is an
educated and independent modern girl. The conflict
between them brings out Shaw's theme that prostitution
is a by-product of capitalist society. No subject could have
been less likely to appeal to the commercial theater of the
day. Furthermore, the censor refused *Mrs. Warren* a license for production. Eight years later it was produced
by a society which, having the status of a club, could give
private performances. The critics greeted it with a howl.
It was subsequently performed in New York, where the
police arrested the entire company. In the trial which followed, the conclusion was reached that vice had not been

made attractive and that the play was worth production. If such scenes, however, could arise more than ten years after the creation of *Mrs. Warren*, it was no wonder that the play did nothing for its author when it was completed.

Mrs. Warren was too far in advance of her day. Shaw perceived this and, because he was bent on success, tried again in a different spirit. Florence Farr, with whom Shaw was still intimate, was entrusted with the management of the Avenue Theatre in London to produce a series of plays, her backer being a certain Miss Horniman, whose wealth, judiciously applied, did much to foster a renaissance of drama in England and Ireland. Immediately Shaw started to write a play for Florence, and none too soon. Her first production was a failure, and she had been driven to talk of reviving *Widowers' Houses*. But *Arms and the Man* was finished with speed and opened, after frantic rehearsals, in April, 1894.

When Shaw came to publish his early plays, he put them in two volumes entitled *Plays Pleasant* and *Plays Unpleasant*. *Arms and the Man* is the earliest of the pleasant ones. To Shaw's intense annoyance it was later made into a light opera with which he firmly refused to have anything to do. It is a satire on military glory and, once more, on romantic love. And unlike the *Plays Unpleasant*, it is really funny. But these were the days before two world wars when military glory was not a thing to laugh at. Shaw had placed his scene in Bulgaria, but one of the actors on the first night by a slip of the tongue spoke of the *British* army. It passed almost unnoticed, but when the author appeared amid applause at the end of the performance, someone in the gallery let out a hearty "Boo!" As usual, Shaw was equal to the occasion.

"I quite agree with you, my friend," he said, "but what can we two do against a whole houseful of the opposite opinion?"

This was all very well at the time, but the play made enemies. The Prince of Wales, who had been induced to go, was so angry that he stormed out in the middle. He said the author must be mad. The actors, meanwhile, as they became more used to the play, began to insert the romantic innuendoes to which they were accustomed, thereby spoiling the comic effect. The play ran for eleven weeks and steadily lost money.

At least *Arms and the Man* had been presented to the public. Encouraged by this glimmer of success, Shaw was already at work on his best and most characteristic play of this early period. *Candida* is his answer to Ibsen's *A Doll's House* and treats of the same theme. Ibsen's Nora, however, is an innocent woman who grows up during the play to assert her own judgment. Candida, married to a socialist clergyman, a popular orator and spellbinder, has always known she is the stronger of the two. When events bring this fact into the open, she stays with her husband because he needs her, gently showing the poet who has idealized her that she has feet of clay after all. Candida is a woman both modern in her ideas and age-old in her practice. Shaw's difficulty in getting this play produced lay not in the sympathy attracted by the leading character, who conquered hearts from the first. Actor-managers, however, could find no male part of equal stature. Both the poet and the clergyman, though sympathetic to a certain degree, expose their weaknesses. Leading actors could not see themselves in either part, though one did offer to play the poet if he could be made blind to attract more sympathy. Two years and a half were to pass before the Independent Theatre gave *Candida* a single performance in Aberdeen. Three years later still, the Stage Society performed it twice in London.

Meanwhile, "Corno di Bassetto," who had been going on his merry way for about six years, seized a chance to make his final bow at the end of 1894. Perhaps Shaw had said all he wanted to on music. In any case, his interest was focusing on the drama; and an opportunity came up to write a weekly drama column in *The Saturday Review* for a slightly increased wage.

Shaw's interest in the theater had dated from his Dublin days when the investment of a shilling for a cheap seat at the play was not thought wasteful in a family where shillings were not easily come by. Even in London during the period when his purse was emptiest, he had squandered money on the theater when he possessed it. By 1895, when he was writing plays himself, he had formed opinions about what ought to be done and how to do it.

The king of the theatrical world at this time was Henry Irving, actor-manager of the Lyceum. Irving was an actor in the old style, compelling attention by the sheerest strength of personality. But in order to project himself across the footlights, he needed a play tailored to fit him. No melodrama was too banal if it gave him opportunities. Shakespeare was unscrupulously cut to suit his purpose.

Ellen Terry, beloved actress.

All this irritated Shaw, who had grown up on Shakespeare and was far more familiar with his unexpurgated text than most men. But worse than all was Irving's treatment of his leading lady.

Ellen Terry was London's darling, a great actress as delightful off-stage as on. Since Irving cared little whether she got good roles unless these served to feed his own, London too often saw her in plays which were unworthy of her powers. It happened, moreover, that Shaw had lost his heart to Ellen Terry.

Their correspondence had started by a letter of hers to *The Star* about a young musical protégée. Ellen Terry was remarkable for her kindness of heart and gave freely of time and money to help others. "Corno di Bassetto" took the trouble to go and hear the young lady in question and to write Ellen a long appreciation of her talents and the best way to cultivate them. Once started, the series of letters soon became more intimate.

They had never met — or rather they had once done so in a crowd, but Ellen did not remember Shaw. Now neither one felt the need of an introduction. Together they were building a glittering castle in the air in which Ellen figured as an enchanting princess whom he adored. Both felt that a meeting might spoil the precious illusion.

Letters grew longer and more confidential. By 1896, Shaw was writing to Ellen every few days, telling her everything he felt. She in her turn asked his advice, sending him for instance an example of the begging letters for which she was too easy a mark. More cynical than she, he responded that the tale was too beautifully told and must have been rehearsed. He advised her that the amateur beggar never begs well. He might have applied the same verdict to his own letters.

Stripped of its charm and its endearments, this famous correspondence between two people who chose to love at a distance is seen to be in essence practical. Shaw wanted Ellen to act in more modern plays, and he was qualified to help her in various situations. Not that the love expressed is mere embroidery. It meant something to them both; yet each understood its limitations, so that they were perfectly easy with one another. He could even talk to her about his other loves:

> I am fond of women . . . , but I am in earnest
> about quite other things . . . Love is only diver-
> sion and recreation to me . . . It is . . . why I
> act the lover so diabolically well that even the
> women who are clever enough to understand
> that such a person as myself might exist cannot
> bring themselves to believe that I am that person.

Pretty soon, the drama critic of *The Saturday Review*
had developed a promising feud with Henry Irving. It
galled him to see the talents of London's greatest actor
wasted on old-fashioned drama, and he never ceased to
reproach him about Ellen.

> When I think of the originality and modernity of
> the talent she revealed twenty years ago, and of
> its remorseless waste ever since in "supporting"
> an actor who prefers *The Iron Chest* to Ibsen,
> my regard for Sir Henry Irving cannot blind me
> to the fact that it would have been better for us
> twenty-five years ago to have tied him up in a
> sack with every existing copy of the works of
> Shakespeare and dropped him into the crater of
> the nearest volcano.

He had written a drama for Ellen Terry, a curtain-
raiser about Napoleon and a mysterious lady which he
wanted Irving to act with her. Irving, however, preferred
to offer fifty pounds for the right to produce it when it was
convenient to do so. Shaw retorted that he did not wish
his early efforts to be postponed until they looked shabby
in comparison with his later work. Moreover his goodwill
as a critic was not to be bought by fifty pounds and a half-

promise. This implication was offensive to Irving, already annoyed by his persistent critic. Matters became worse when Shaw commented on carelessness in a performance in terms which, Irving thought, implied that he was drunk. Shaw in fact had no such suspicion, but Irving, who knew that he really had been drunk, was resentful. "Your Mr. Pshaw!" he said disdainfully to Ellen.

In November, 1896, she peeped through the curtain of the Lyceum to see the critic of *The Saturday Review* in the stalls. "And so that was you!" she wrote next day. "How deadly delicate you look!" She had not realized how pale and thin he was.

This much reality did not destroy the illusion. Ellen was relying on him heavily. When she had to struggle with Imogen in Irving's revival of *Cymbeline*, he gave her detailed advice which was a remarkable tribute to his own Shakespearean knowledge. When she went on tour, when financial troubles began to overwhelm the Lyceum, Shaw was ready to tell her what to do. As a hostess who entertained him said of him later on:

> Before you know where you are, he has chosen a school for your son, made your will for you, regulated your diet, assumed all the privileges of your family solicitor, your housekeeper, your clergyman, your doctor, your dressmaker, your hairdresser, and your estate agent . . . And when he can find nothing more to do, he goes away and forgets all about you.

It was all true, except that he did not forget Ellen Terry.

1889–1898

Courtship and Marriage

THE UNEXPECTED success of *Fabian Essays* was due to
the fact that the problems of an industrial civilization
were widely recognized among people to whom revolutionary socialism made no appeal. The Fabians, though
socialists, were prepared to construct their ideal state on
present foundations. To them, the socialist state was the
welfare state; and they saw it already partially in operation wherever a municipality put up a gasworks or organized a system of public transportation. Thus though the
Fabians saw each reform as part of a larger whole, they
were in general on the side of all reformers. They had
something for everybody.

Among those who read this famous classic with approval
was Beatrice Potter, one of the nine daughters of a prom-
inent railroad industrialist. The Potter girls were intelligent as well as rich, so that most of them had married
coming men. Beatrice, however, was already nearly thirty
and been hard to please. She was handsome in a striking
way with pale complexion, aquiline features, and fine
eyebrows shading bright brown eyes. As a personality she

was too formidable to please many, yet she was a skillful hostess and had managed her father's house for a number of years. Joseph Chamberlain, perhaps the most forceful politician of his day, had wooed her; but Beatrice had not been interested in forwarding a husband's career. She wanted to use her own talents.

Beatrice had turned her attention to the conditions of the working class, partly because her family, which had risen rapidly, still retained its working-class connections. It was fashionable in those days to do good to the deserving poor, but Beatrice aspired to something more fundamental. Charles Booth, who had married a cousin, asked her to help him amass the facts for his monumental *Life and Labor in London*, one of the earliest pieces of detailed research into working-class conditions. On her own account, Beatrice published an essay on dock life in East London, which was followed by a series on sweated labor, for the purpose of which she had herself trained as a pants presser and worked in a sweatshop.

By 1889, she was gathering material for a book on the British cooperative movement; and she happened to mention to a friend the difficulty of getting reliable information. "Sidney Webb, one of the Fabian essayists, is your man," replied the other. "He knows everything; when you go out for a walk with him, he literally pours out information."

Thus encouraged, Beatrice got in touch with Sidney Webb. To her diary she confided the details of his undistinguished appearance, not forgetting to notice "a most bourgeois black coat, shiny with wear." But she liked him. She commented on his direct speech, his open-mind-edness, his warmth of heart. "He has the self-assurance of one who is always thinking faster than his neighbors; who is untroubled by doubts; and to whom the acquisition of facts is as easy as the grasping of things; but he has no vanity and is totally unselfconscious." Presently she was introduced to the Fabians and found them a group like-minded with herself. She began to ask its unmarried members down to her father's place for weekends. Obe-diently they all went, save Bernard Shaw. He insisted later that she was looking them all over as possible hus-bands and that he already knew Sidney was in love. Be that as it may, the engagement of Beatrice and Sidney followed in due course.

Beatrice's diary calls it a working compact between two socialists, which may seem a curious way of beginning a completely happy marriage in which neither grew out of love. Both felt, however, that the work they were doing was more important than themselves. Beatrice's income allowed them to devote their lives to their cause, produc-ing a series of epoch-making books and creating a true cen-ter of progressive thought. Cabinet ministers were glad to dine with the Webbs, and Sidney became an unofficial adviser to many a politician or government expert. Start-ing in the nineties, the Fabian Society exerted through the Webbs a powerful influence which culminated in 1945 in the Labour Government with two hundred and twenty-nine Fabians in power, including forty-one in the Cabinet. The welfare state in Great Britain today is Fa-bian work.

The marriage of Beatrice and Sidney did not take place till 1892 because Beatrice insisted on waiting until the death of her father, who was bedridden from a stroke. She knew quite well that her successful sisters would be outraged at her choice, as indeed they were. Privately they christened Sidney "the gnome," and one of Beatrice's nephews confided to a friend that "Aunt Bo is going to marry a seditious cockney cad." Since Aunt Bo was now thirty-two, however, and Sidney did not care what the Potters thought, the marriage took place without further delay. It happened, therefore, that in the very year in

Sidney Webb, "the ablest man in England," and Beatrice Webb.

which *Widowers' Houses* was produced for the first time, the political side of Shaw's work was seriously affected by a new relationship.

Beatrice was a vehement woman. Her enemies called her bossy. At all events, she liked to lay down the law and had no sense of humor. Shaw's flippancies annoyed and puzzled her, while his usual methods of charming a woman could not be applied to Sidney's wife. "It is enormously to her credit," he points out, "that she forced herself to have me in the house because I was Sidney's loyalest and most useful friend." In the course of years each became an old habit with the other so that they hardly knew that they were not the dearest of friends. In the meantime, however, though Shaw's intercourse with Sidney Webb was in no way interrupted, he went through a painful process of readjustment.

There was a great deal going on. In 1891 came a general election in which Shaw and Webb imposed their program on the Liberal Party by dubious methods. A certain Mr. Beale, a Liberal candidate who had no chance at the polls, was selected as their victim. Shaw attended a very small meeting with a string of resolutions drafted by Sidney Webb. He moved their passage. A reading was demanded, and he read them, "turning over Webb's pages by batches and not reading most of them." Mr. Beale, unaware of what was being done, seconded them. They were passed unanimously. That night Shaw sent them down to *The Star*, together with the report of a speech on them which Mr. Beale was said to have delivered. "Next day he [Beale] found the National Liberal Club in an uproar at his revolutionary break-away. But he played up; buttoned his coat determinedly; said we lived in progressive times and must move with them; and carried it off." All the papers took up the so-called Newcastle program; and Mr. Gladstone, the Liberal leader, who had no vital issues to put forward, perceived the importance of giving it his blessing. The Liberals got in; but not unnaturally they made no effort to carry out the program. The Fabians countered in 1892 with another remarkable pamphlet entitled "To Your Tents, O Israel." Each of the government departments was examined to find what it had done about the Newcastle program. All were seen to be lacking. The Fabians thereupon called on the working classes to form a political party of their own. The Independent Labour Party was the result of this maneuver, though the more important Labour Party was not founded until 1906.

Sidney Webb, meanwhile, had obtained a seat on the London County Council and was directing its Technical Education Board, which controlled all education in London, except in Greek and theology. He was busy increasing secondary education and giving life to the University of London. But Sidney's written style was banal, and he depended heavily upon Shaw in producing the informative pamphlets for which the Fabians were becoming known. By the turn of the century they had published a hundred, all the best of which had at least been edited by Shaw, while many others were indebted to him for turns of phrase or important suggestions. Meanwhile, in a single year the Fabians delivered well over three thou-

Shaw aged thirty-six in 1892.

sand lectures, despite the fact that they still had hardly more than a hundred members.

Now that she and Sidney Webb were so happily married, Beatrice was not above trying a little matchmaking for other Fabians. Why should not, for instance, Olivier and Wallas marry money and devote their entire time to Fabian work? Beatrice had a wide circle of distinguished acquaintances and was always glad to admit young men and women of talent into her group. However, her innocent efforts to pair people off were not ambitious enough to include Bernard Shaw. Beatrice, who was not flirtatious, was less tolerant than Sidney of Shaw's ways with a woman. She had to convince herself that he was not like other people and must not be judged in her usual fashion. By so doing, she put him outside the pale and never considered that he could feel deeply at all. Thus when she first discovered Charlotte Payne-Townshend, Beatrice thought her a suitable bride for Graham Wallas.

Charlotte Payne-Townshend was of Irish extraction, a distant cousin of that very Uniacke Townsend in whose office Shaw had started his career. Her father was a wealthy landowner who had the misfortune to marry a woman so discontented and so demanding that she was nearly impossible to live with. Indeed, the poor man eventually died, so his daughter was convinced, of sheer unhappiness. Charlotte had made up her mind to remain single because married life as she had seen it was nothing but misery. This resolution, however, forced her to stay with her mother and attempt to bear with her. Charlotte did her duty as best she could, but when in her mid-thirties she found herself free and well-to-do, she felt relief. It took her, however, some time to find a life for herself. Her mother had hated Ireland, and Charlotte was now too remote from its problems to be able to settle down where she had been born. She had learned to like travel and was not used to feeling at home anywhere. Her sister had married years before. No place or person had special claims upon her.

Charlotte Payne-Townshend was not a beautiful woman. Her face was too square for that, her features too blunt, her complexion too sallow. But she had abundant bright brown hair and striking eyes of a palish green. Dressed properly — and she had learned to dress well — she could look handsome. She was not so much educated as cultured, spoke various languages and was accustomed to hold her own among intelligent people. Alas, one of the things she did with her new freedom was to fall in love with a Swedish doctor who was fashionable at Rome and had ladies on his list who were socially superior to Charlotte Payne-Townshend. Instead of finding her niche in the world, she broke her heart.

It was healing slowly when she met the Fabians. That sense of duty which had bidden her stick by her mother had given her an interest in social problems. Notwithstanding, she seemed a fish out of water among the Fabians; and she might simply have passed on to other things if Beatrice had not been interested in her money.

Sidney Webb had been left ten thousand pounds in 1894, and he was using half of it to found a school for economic studies which has become famous as the London School of Economics. It started in two rooms on a ground floor, and Miss Payne-Townshend helped by renting the top of the house for an apartment. In addition, she endowed a woman's scholarship. If she had been allowed to do so, she would have liked to be a doctor, so that she took pleasure in opening professional training for other young women.

Matters were at this stage when summer came around, and the Sidney Webbs went off on holiday. In other words, they got away from the distractions of London and settled down in peace to some good, hard work.

It was their practice to rent a country vicarage, which was usually some immense old ark, where in moderate discomfort they could have their friends to stay, including that unattached old bachelor Bernard Shaw, who was freed from his slavery to theaters and first nights in the summer season. On this occasion, Beatrice suggested to Miss Payne-Townshend that they should join forces and rent a vicarage in Wales together.

Shaw came, but he did not enjoy himself with the Webbs. He was tired, for one thing. His dizzying round of activities during the nineties was never-ending. To Ellen Terry in 1898 he complains of a single fortnight when he had three first nights to attend, two County Council election meetings to speak at, one Fabian executive meeting, four other committees, a pamphlet to write, a novel to adapt in order to secure drama rights in it for a friend, an article, his usual occasional headache, and proofs of his book, which were the more exacting because he dealt in person with the printer and was endlessly particular about type. Meanwhile, his personal life was as hectic as ever. The production of his plays had introduced him to actresses. Janet Achurch, for instance, had made a sensation in Ibsen's *A Doll's House* and was the person whom he wished to play Candida. Janet was married, and Shaw had been careful not to make her husband jealous. Short of this, however, his interest in her was great. He immersed himself in her problems, which included drink, morphia, and an attack of typhoid, and was ready to spend ages improving her acting style.

It always was easier for him to attract new ladies than to cast old ones off.

When he went to stay with the Webbs in summer, Shaw felt lonely. Their life was systematic. Long hours of it were spent in work, and he had to watch Beatrice "every now and then when she needed a refresher (Sidney was tireless) rise from her chair, throw away her pen, and hurl herself on her husband in a shower of caresses which lasted until the passion for work resumed its sway." These honeymoon habits embarrassed or bored him. To his own astonishment he records, "I — I, George Bernard Shaw, — have actually suffered from something which in anyone else I should call unhappiness." He hated the feeling of being always on guard with Beatrice. They embarrassed one another when they found themselves alone without some subject of immediate interest to discuss. It was hard for him to feel self-conscious in the relationship, or to look on at married happiness from outside.

Afternoons at the Webbs' were devoted to exercise. In those days before the automobile, the bicycle was all the rage among young and active people. Bernard Shaw, who always thought of himself as a nervous specimen without much physical courage, was a mad cyclist. Over and over again he risked his life by putting up his feet in the days before free-wheelers and tearing down hill around blind curves as though possessed. Nor was he without his share of accidents. A collision with Bertrand Russell left him a wreck for about two days. "I am not thoroughly convinced yet," he writes, "that I was not killed. Anybody but a vegetarian would have been. Nobody but a teetotaller would have faced a bicycle again for six months."

After these strenuous pursuits, in the evenings, the Webbs and their guests talked shop. In other words, they argued, Shaw matching his brilliance against Sidney's encyclopedic knowledge. It was animated, even exciting; but it was not restful. The green-eyed Miss Payne-Townshend was astonished to find that next morning at breakfast the parties who had been shouting at one another all evening were quite reconciled.

Other guests came and went, but Shaw and Miss Payne-Townshend were permanent fixtures. He found it a relief to sit up talking to her when Beatrice and Sidney had gone to their well-earned rest at a sensible hour. He even wrote to Ellen Terry about her and called her "my green-eyed millionairess." Charlotte listened well, was, if not intellectual, at least intelligent. Still parading her own broken heart, she was not over-eager to fall in love with him. On the whole he liked her, and she was a comfort to him. Perhaps he had never needed comforting before.

Summer passed and, tired as he was, he plunged once more into his activities in London. He was elected to the vestry, or in other words the borough council of St. Pancras, the district of London in which he lived. The meetings of this prosaic body were electrified by his presence, and after his usual fashion he spared neither effort nor time. Every so often one realizes from his letters to Ellen Terry that as he rushes between committees and visits to the British Museum he is dropping in at Adelphi Terrace, Miss Payne-Townshend's commodious flat above the London School of Economics. He even passes by on his way home after an evening at the theater, just to see if Miss Payne-Townshend is still up. He goes on home, where he works until the small hours, protecting his eyes with a shade and using green, non-glare paper because they are weary. He has difficulty in hearing his alarm the next morning and thinks he is lazy. Only occasionally does he admit he is bone-tired.

He had determined that, if he could not get his plays acted, they should at least be read. He was preparing to issue them in two volumes: *Plays Unpleasant* and *Plays Pleasant*. The work that this entailed took extra time.

He was not content to publish acting copies with a few stage directions where they were desperately needed. To be read, a play must at least approach the form of a novel. Accordingly, he was providing detailed descriptions of scenes and characters, together with stage directions conveying not merely actions, but expressions or even the feelings of the moment. In other words, he was rewriting the whole set of his past plays, as well as adding the prefaces which became so characteristic of his work. These introductions were articles or sermons, highly personal, just as his critical work had been, and discussed the theme of the play or else some issue which had been suggested by it. For instance, the preface to *Mrs. Warren's Profession* explained and commented upon his battles with the British censor.

He had learned from the socialist artist William Morris

to care about the design of his typescript and the look of his page. To a man with his restless energy and desire for artistic perfection a publisher was a man who sold books wholesale, not by any means a person to take charge of the relations which ought to exist between an author and his printer. For this reason, the publishing of Shaw's books involved labor which an author seldom undertakes. Every decision on the size of the margins, the spacing of words or lines, the indentations, and of course about the paper, type, and binding was made by him.

Charlotte Payne-Townshend had found something to do. The green-eyed millionairess had become "my secretary." She had taught herself to type and to decipher his neat shorthand. She did not pretend she was not fond of him, but she still preserved her independence. It was he who had learned to rely on her. "Do you forsake *all* your duties, even those of secretary?" he writes in 1897. "I send you instructions to arrive at eleven and *wait* for you . . . so perfect is my faith in your arrival. I get your shawl and your foot warmer. I sweep the hearth to make the fire look nice for you." But Charlotte had gone to Belgium with a friend. She had asked him to come as well, but he had poured scorn on the notion of his chaperoning two ladies. He had imagined that this would settle the question of her going at all, but he had been wrong.

The 1894 production of *Arms and the Man* had been attended by an American actor named Richard Mansfield, who was tempted by the leading part. He hesitated because the hero is off-stage for almost the whole of Act Two, but eventually he decided to acquire the American rights. He put on an inexpensive production in New York with no great success. The play, however, was part of his repertoire by now; and he revived it later on with better fortune. A welcome trickle of American royalties inspired Shaw to tackle an American theme. *The Devil's Disciple* was a melodrama written with Mansfield in mind and composed, to waste no time, while Shaw was sitting for his portrait.

The Devil's Disciple is not one of Shaw's greatest plays. Its plot is stuffed with melodrama like any bad western — the sacrifice of a man's life for another, the court-martial, the gallows, the eleventh-hour reprieve. It reads well, however, and acts well. The characters are subtly developed, and the motives of the Devil's Disciple become more interesting as we see why they are not romantic. The wit of Burgoyne mocks at conventional codes of military honor. In fact, the play is provocative as well as simple. Its American theme appealed naturally to an American audience, and Mansfield's production was an enormous success in New York. For the first time Shaw received more money than would satisfy his day-to-day wants. If he really had wished to marry his green-eyed millionairess, one of the difficulties in the way was now removed. He had always felt he would lose his independence if he were forced to depend on his wife's money.

All the same he did not want to marry Charlotte. The summer arrangement between the Webbs and Miss Payne-Townshend had continued in the following years so that Beatrice had an exceptional chance to form her opinion about what was going on. In 1897, she thought the affair was drawing to an end. "He has been flattered by her devotion and absorption in him; he is kindly and has a cat-like preference for those people to whom he is accustomed. But there are ominous signs that he is tired of watching the effect of little words of gallantry." Beatrice was still convinced that he had no heart to lose. Perhaps he felt the same himself. At all events, that summer things came to a climax between him and Charlotte. He confided to Ellen:

> There was a sort of earthquake because she had been cherishing a charming project of making me a very generous and romantic proposal — saving it up as a sort of climax to the proofs she was giving me every day of her regard for me. When I received that golden moment with shuddering horror and wildly asked the fare to Australia, she was inexpressibly taken aback and her pride, which is considerable, was much startled.

Poor Charlotte! Yet she could not entirely keep away, and he could not do without her.

A fresh development arose in 1898. The Webbs were going to travel this year, and Charlotte wished to go with them. Shaw would not take the time and said that he could not afford it. He stayed at home. For the last twenty-two years he had been living with his mother. His sister Lucy, whose career had not after all been very successful, had married and quit the stage. By this time she was separated from her husband and lived alone.

Lucinda Elizabeth had long ago given up trying to rent

an entire house. She and her son were established in their usual discomfort on the top floor of 29 Fitzroy Square, where each managed to live a separate life. Shaw's time was chiefly spent in his little study, almost filled by a typewriter, table, and chair. Since his window was always wide open, London smuts drifted in upon papers or books, which were left open wherever he happened to stop reading. Manuscripts, proofs, or letters lay heaped under and over sugar bowls, butter dishes, apples, cups of cocoa, half-finished plates of porridge, or blackened saucepans. He never sat down to a meal with his mother, but every so often a sloppy maid brought up a half-cold egg or removed some of the debris of previous meals. Nobody tidied this sanctum except its owner, who seldom undertook the task because it consumed two entire days, which he could not often spare.

Charlotte and the Webbs had barely started on their journey before Shaw, striding about London in his usual haste, got a sore place on his foot from a too-tight shoe. He ignored it, and pretty soon he developed an abscess which inflamed the entire leg. The doctor who opened it diagnosed necrosis of the bone and was horrified at the general condition of his patient. Too much activity had too long been sustained on an inadequate diet. It had sounded all very well when Shaw wrote to a hostess: "I can make as good a dinner off brown bread and cheese and an apple or any handy fruit as if I had Mark Antony's kitchen at my disposal." Now at last his rundown condition made him seriously ill. Since he could not get about to visit his vegetarian restaurants, his food became more limited than ever. Forced inactivity fretted his nerves. So alarmed were his friends that Graham Wallas wired an account of his condition to the Webbs.

Traveling with the Webbs was not mere recreation. They were at present in Rome, where Charlotte was studying municipal conditions. She was past forty and beyond the stage of maiden bashfulness, so that she had no hesitation in taking the first train home.

Charlotte arrived in London and hastened to 29 Fitzroy Square. She was appalled. Not only was Shaw obviously ill, but he was living in the most neglected conditions. Lucinda Elizabeth, who had her own work to perform, simply left her son to look after himself. Charlotte took in the grim and dirty apartment, the peeling wallpaper, the squalid little study, the unkempt maid, and the inadequate meals. Forthwith she laid down the law. She was going to hire a house, install him in it, and see that he was properly looked after. He could not — and he must make up his mind to the fact — recover under these conditions.

He knew that she was right; indeed he had already thought he was going to die. He was not afraid of death, but he was willing to be talked into living. It touched him to find that Charlotte cared so much that he should do so. But he would not live with Charlotte unless he married her. It was unthinkable that he should involve her and the Fabians in scandal.

Both found their objections to marriage evaporating.

He had resisted her because he valued a freedom which he now saw he had lost in any case. She had discovered that her purpose in life was looking after him. Well, she was forty and he forty-two and devotion was a quiet, comforting thing. He thought it a better foundation for marriage than a devouring passion.

On June 1, 1898, they were married in a civil ceremony. Shaw turned up as he was in an ancient jacket which his crutches had worn right through. "The registrar never imagined that I could possibly be the bridegroom," he recounted later. "He took me for the inevitable beggar who completes all wedding processions. Wallas, over six feet tall, was so obviously the hero of the occasion that the registrar was on the point of marrying him to my betrothed. But Wallas, thinking the formula rather too strong for a mere witness, hesitated at the last moment and left the prize to me."

He might have been too ill to buy new clothes, but his spirits were always equal to a jest. Anonymously he sent the following notice to *The Star*:

> As a lady and gentleman were out driving in Henrietta Street, Covent Garden yesterday, a heavy shower drove them to take shelter in the office of the Superintendent Registrar there, and in the confusion of the moment he married them. The lady was an Irish lady named Miss Payne-Townshend, and the gentleman was George Bernard Shaw . . . Startling as was the liberty undertaken by the Henrietta Street official, it turns

out well. Miss Payne-Townshend is an Irish lady with an income many times the volume of that which "Corno di Bassetto" used to earn, but to that happy man, being a vegetarian, the circumstance is of no moment.

In such fashion he avenged his capture by the green-eyed millionairess.

1904–1907

The Court Theater

"MY SITUATION," wrote Bernard Shaw, tongue in cheek, "is a solemn one. Life is offered me on condition of eating beefsteaks. My weeping family crowd about me with Bovril and Brand's Essence. But death is better than cannibalism. My will contains directions for my funeral, which will be followed not by mourning coaches, but by herds of oxen, sheep, swine, flocks of poultry, and a small traveling aquarium of live fish, all wearing white scarves in honor of the man who perished rather than eat his fellow creatures."

By his weeping family, he meant quite simply Charlotte, who urged that his prejudices should be put aside in matters of life and death. Her husband clung to his vegetarian diet, not really because death was better than cannibalism, but because he was certain that he knew more than the doctor. Had he not confidently made out a diet list for Janet Achurch when she was brought to the verge of death by typhoid? Had he not conceded to her husband that if she could not bear woolen sheets, well, people had occasionally got better in linen?

Charlotte was doing her best. She had rented a house in the country, hired appropriate help, and instructed her cook in nourishing vegetarian dishes. But Bernard Shaw was not an easy patient. Less than three weeks after the marriage he decided to go upstairs for a book he wanted, instead of summoning assistance. Coming down, he slipped on his crutch and fell headlong to the floor, which was paved with flagstones, breaking his left arm above the wrist. No sooner had he recovered somewhat from this accident than he tried to work off his nervous energy by riding a bicycle with one foot. He fell over, sprained his ankle badly, and had to be confined to a wheelchair. Another operation was performed on his foot, so that he impatiently asked for a radical amputation which would have left him permanently lame. Eventually he was better again, but twice more sprained his ankle in frantic efforts to get about. After nearly a year, it was discovered that iodoform gauze, which was being packed into his wound in accordance with Lister's antiseptic theories, had prevented it healing. As he recovered, his skeptical attitude towards the learning of doctors was increased.

He had given up his job as dramatic critic because he was too ill to do the work. In any case, he was tired of it and did not need the money. He had been forced also to interrupt his habit of speaking on Sundays and evenings. By now he had become so popular a speaker that societies lucky enough to get him recouped their finances by charging entrance fees. As a consequence, his working-class audiences were becoming smaller than his middle-class ones. It was now logical to reserve his speeches for important occasions.

Ill or well, however, he had to write. In that first year of marriage when he was banging and bumping himself in desperate efforts to resume his active life, he was busy writing his first play on a grand scale. *Caesar and Cleopatra* is a study of human greatness; it carries through in more detail the ideas of his playlet about Napoleon. The political side of Shaw admires Caesar as the perfect man of action. Caesar's judgment is superior, and therefore he is able to ride above problems of conduct which confuse lesser men. Needing to deceive, he does not condescend to lie because he knows how to take advantage of his enemies' mistrust. Determined to be master, he has no use for vengeance because he perceives that this leads on to further vengeance. Desiring to seize the lighthouse of Alexandria, he releases his opponents so that they may divert their army to the saving of the burning library. For his own part, Caesar thinks the records of the past are not important, compared to laying foundations for the future. In sum, Caesar has the virtues which make men love him. They are genuine, yet like an accomplished housewife he knows how to use the last scrap of them to his advantage. This is not mere economical instinct; it is wisdom. Among his fellow creatures, he stands alone. "I have found flocks and pastures, men and cities, but no other Caesar, no air native to me, no man kindred to me, none who can do my day's deed, and think my night's thought."

In contrast to Caesar, Cleopatra is childish, instinc-

tively vicious, and yet with a spark of grandeur. Nothing
that Cleopatra does will escape notice, and much will attract admiration; but the loves and hates which she in-
spires are on a sensual level.

The play in which these characters are presented is
neither a comedy nor a tragedy. Its plot is nothing more
than a device for revealing Caesar and does not develop
him in any way. Thus *Caesar and Cleopatra* resembles
the old chronicle play to which Shakespeare gave life in
his historical series. Nothing memorable had been done
with this since Shakespeare's time; but in Shaw's hands it
acquired a new and cheerful irreverence. Britannus,
Caesar's British slave, is a deliberate caricature of the
Victorian Englishman. When Cleopatra inquires: "Is it
true that when Caesar caught you on that island, you
were painted all over blue?" he answers solemnly: "Blue
is the colour worn by all Britons of good standing. In
war we stain our bodies blue; so that though our enemies
may strip us of our clothes, they cannot strip us of our
respectability." In similar anachronistic vein, Apollodorus
the art dealer cries: "Art for Art's sake!" Caesar's opponents invent the slogan: "Egypt for the Egyptians!"

Caesar and Cleopatra is a highly original work
crammed with excitement and made vivid by the excellence of its character drawing. It is a far cry, however,
from the socialist plays like *Mrs. Warren's Profession,*
or even from the critique of marriage contained in *Candida.* Shaw is a man of many facets, and it remains to be
seen how far the reformer and the artist in him go hand
in hand.

Shaw's published plays were by now widely read; but despite his success in New York, he could not yet make money in London. In 1897, a delightful farce called *You Never Can Tell* had been accepted by a commercial theater; but the rehearsals had gone so badly that the play was withdrawn. In 1899, the London Stage Society was organized to produce the best works of contemporary playwrights in private performances, distinguished actors offering their services free. In this fashion *You Never Can Tell* was at last produced, followed by several others, including *Captain Brassbound's Conversion,* which Shaw had written especially for the aging Ellen Terry. Ellen had not admired her play at first and only gradually came around to see how like she was to Lady Cecily. Irving could not be got to take an interest in the less attractive part of Captain Brassbound. Ellen, however, attended the Stage Society performance in 1900, and she was introduced to the author with whom she had for eight years corresponded.

They were no longer as intimate as they had been. It stood to reason that Shaw confided in Charlotte instead of pouring out his feelings to Ellen. All the same, he was glad to advise her still. She was getting elderly, and Irving's theater was running into debt. In a few years she would be asking Shaw for parts, and he would be putting her off. Before this happened, however, she did at least get her chance in *Captain Brassbound.*

Married life had settled into its routine. Charlotte was not a housewife, nor had she any particular taste. She liked to be comfortable, however, and had the knack

of keeping good servants. Her flat in Adelphi Terrace was not convenient or modern, but it was in a block of eighteenth-century houses and boasted one of the handsomest doorways in London. Her upstairs living-room windows looked over the Thames to the Surrey Hills, while, on either side, St. Paul's and the Houses of Parliament framed her view. Shaw's own study was a small working room on the fourth floor, but except in size it bore little resemblance to his room at his mother's. Now that he was well looked after, he had taken to tidy ways which matched his neat handwriting. Charlotte saw that he was punctual to meals and that his diet, which she refused to share, was palatable.

He was still too busy with political work — vestry meetings or Fabian committees. Both he and Charlotte felt the need of a country place as a refuge from London. They rented several houses and finally in 1904 established themselves in the Old Vicarage, Ayot St. Lawrence, a vast and rather ugly red brick building in an unspoiled village not too far from London. Here Shaw found in the churchyard the gravestone of a woman of eighty with the motto on it: "Her time was short." This encouraged him, he said, to think favorably of the climate. Actually, once established, he hated to move, though Charlotte never liked Ayot. No sooner did they come down from the London apartment than, it seemed to him, Charlotte was planning to travel.

Charlotte was an inveterate traveler. She liked a change of scene; and she saw the necessity of getting her husband away so that his activities could not once more

Charlotte Shaw, the green-eyed millionairess.

drive him into a breakdown. As he became famous, pressures on him increased to a terrible extent. Charlotte's remedy did indeed force him to take vacations. Its drawback was that he did not like travel, and he took his writing with him wherever he went. Indignantly he wrote to his friends from abroad, complaining of scenery, weather, hotels, and snappishness with Charlotte. Twice a year or more, he was forced into traveling somewhere; and it was not as easy as it had once been to write in strange places. He was a celebrity now, and people pursued him.

The performances of the Stage Society had introduced Shaw to a twenty-three-year-old actor, Harley Granville-Barker, who, as he instantly saw, was the very man to play the poet in *Candida*. Barker, who had been brought up to the stage and had been acting since he was eleven, had considerable talents and turned about this time to writing plays and to production. In addition, both he and Shaw were on the management committee of the Stage Society, which had decided to produce the long-censored *Mrs. Warren's Profession*. As a private club it had the right to do so, but it proved by no means easy to hire a stage. Thirteen theaters, three hotels, and two picture galleries refused to have anything to do with the project. The Royal Society of British Artists consented at last to lend its gallery, but canceled permission when it found that one performance was to be on a Sunday. *Mrs. Warren* was eventually performed at the New Lyric Club without stage or scenery, while Barker took the role of the young lover. As usual, the critics loudly denounced it.

By 1904, Shaw and Barker had worked together for several years in growing intimacy. Barker had produced one play of his own and written another, which was banned but given a Stage Society performance. He had in addition produced some plays for the Society and had gained in reputation thereby. Early in that year, J. E. Vedrenne, manager of the Court Theatre, asked Barker to produce a revival of *The Two Gentlemen of Verona* as part of a series of Shakespeare productions at the Court. Barker agreed on condition that Vedrenne should allow half a dozen matinees of *Candida* at the same time. These were highly successful and made a modest profit which encouraged Vedrenne to go into partnership with Barker for a season of matinees at the Court, starting in October.

In this fashion began the most interesting drama revival in England since Burbage built The Globe in Shakespeare's day. The Vedrenne-Barker management of the Court lasted for three years, comprising nine hundred and eighty-eight performances, of which seven hundred and one were plays by Bernard Shaw. In all, the Court put on eleven Shaw plays, including four new and important ones, so that it very nearly became Shaw's private theater.

He directed these plays himself, and the pains he took in so doing are a measure of his quality. In search of perfection, he never spared himself or other people. It was his usual practice when he had written the first draft of a play to go over the grouping, exits, entrances, and so forth with the aid of chessmen set out on a board. Not until these technical details were worked out to his satisfaction did he consider the play finished. He then tested its effect by reading it aloud to a friend or two, after which he was ready to read it aloud to the cast. He handed out copies, not of the individual roles, as was the custom, but of the entire play to each actor, insisting that all parts be studied in relation to the whole.

He removed himself from the stage; and for a week or so, while the actors stumbled through their lines, he made no interruption, but sat in the front row writing notes with the aid of a flashlight. At the end of each rehearsal, every actor received a page or more of written comments, wittily phrased, but never offensive in tone, suggesting methods of getting more effect out of his lines.

When the actors knew their parts, Shaw began to come up on the stage and interrupt to tell them how to improve their delivery. Lillah McCarthy, who starred at the Court and married Granville-Barker, describes his technique as follows:

> He would tell us how to draw the full value out of a line. He could assume any role, any physical attitude, and make any inflection out of his voice, whether the part was that of an old man, a young man, a budding girl, or an ancient lady. With his amazing hands he would illustrate the mood of the line. We used to watch his hands in wonder. I learned as much from his hands, almost, as from his little notes of correction.

Not all of this was instinctive genius. As part of his career as a speaker, Shaw had studied elocution deliberately. He had also learned voice production from his mother, and he demanded from his actors a contrast of voices, just as he had been used to look for it in opera. His career as dramatic critic had given him wide understanding of what was possible on the stage, and which actors could produce the effects he wanted. His letters to Barker are full of suggestions about casting which reveal his encyclopedic knowledge of the profession.

The trouble he took was almost endless. About a year later, he speaks of his efforts with *Caesar and Cleopatra*, whose Caesar had begged him to "conduct the first rehearsals and settle their business." The result, as he explains,

> is that everything goes on castors: at each rehearsal we take one act, and go through it twice. It goes without a hitch, and we are off in two hours, remarking, if you please, that the play is quite *easy*, and they think that since I only have to prepare an act at a time, it is holiday work for me, whereas with the vestry, the Fabian, the printers (American and English), and a thousand other things, I am working like mad sixteen hours a day.

Among the productions at the Court were four important new plays: *John Bull's Other Island, Man and Superman, Major Barbara,* and *The Doctor's Dilemma*. Bernard Shaw was in his stride at last, and the intelligentsia of London began to take the measure of a really great playwright.

John Bull's Other Island, which opened the Court series, is a comedy about England and Ireland. Plot is unimportant, since so cleverly does Shaw twist the relationships between Englishman, expatriate Irishman, priest, peasant, and "mad" philosopher that the events of the play hardly matter. He had so much to say that Mr. Balfour, who was Prime Minister then and had the reputation of being the wittiest man in Parliament, came to see the play and came again twice more, each time bringing with him one of the leaders of the opposition. He was so funny that Edward VII, who had said the author of *Arms and the Man* was mad, ordered a special performance and broke his chair as he rolled about with laughter — for he was a heavy man.

It was clear by now that Shaw was not writing comedy because he was high-spirited or witty, but because he was an intensely serious man. Satirist as well as comedian, his object was to expose human folly. He approached this task, however, from a fresh angle. Earlier satirists, such as Ben Jonson or Molière, had portrayed the vices of society, while praising its virtues. Their characters had been a miser, a nouveau riche, or a group of conceited women, all people that any man with common sense might disapprove of. Shaw's quarrel was with society as a whole, so that his characters are formed by society and reflect the limitations of their group. His plays abound with clergymen, lawyers, soldiers, doctors, or businessmen, not necessarily bad in themselves, quite often likable, and yet unthinkingly accepting the values of a society shown to be wrong.

No play that Shaw ever wrote displays this tendency more clearly than *The Doctor's Dilemma,* in which Shaw worked off his accumulated spleen against the medical profession. Nothing escapes his eagle eye, from the inherent viciousness of making money out of other men's misfortunes, to the iniquitous system which makes some doctors rich and others poor. None of his five doctors is unbelievable; and even "B.B.," who kills his patient with the appalling confidence of stupidity, is no wicked man. It is the profession in general that Shaw complains of, its ignorance concealed under assurance, its dangerous fads, the contradiction whereby a man whose life is spent in healing hardens his heart to the cruelties of experimentation on animals. The actual dilemma which faces the doctor, whether to save a good man or an unscrupulous artist, is far less clearly analyzed than general problems over which the would-be reformer has brooded long.

Because he aspired to be a prophet, Shaw became a comedian; but he could not confine himself to calling his generation to repentence. The earliest manifesto which he wrote for the Fabians in the eighties had concluded: "we had rather face a Civil War than such another century of suffering as the present one has been." Twenty years later, the Fabians were disillusioned about war and revolution. Socialism, as Shaw now perceived, was no more than political justice, whereas the problems of good and evil pervaded all of nature. Freethinker though he undoubtedly was, Shaw was a religious man; and it was not accident that so many of his great plays had religious themes. To him, the most important need of his times was a positive message.

Man and Superman, performed at the Court in 1905, was Shaw's first full-scale attempt to sum up the meaning of life. On the face of it, he chose a curious framework for this effort. *Man and Superman* is a comedy about the conflict between man as a creative artist and woman as a reproductive instinct. Ann Whitefield has marked down John Tanner as her future husband. He, however, is a "revolutionist," a young Shaw who has written a book and has schemes for human betterment. He loves Ann, but he flees her because he perceives that marriage and children will destroy the impetus to do his work. She pursues. As usual, the true plot lies in the idea; the conflict is developed through a variety of scenes in which comic fancy is more important than probability. Even more completely than before, Shaw's skill in the drama of ideas triumphs over irrelevance or farce. In its own fashion, *Man and Superman* is tightly knit, always excepting a single act which is not often performed.

The idea of this play had been given to Shaw by a friend who had asked him, since he mocked so often at romantic love, to write a play on Don Juan, tradition's great lover. Shaw's answer was this reversal of the battle of the sexes, woman pursuing and attempting to tame man, who tries to escape her. Nevertheless, John Tanner is an English form of Don Juan Tenorio, Ann Whitefield is Doña Ana, and her elderly guardian may play the part of Doña Ana's father. Thus in a dream which is contained in the fourth act of the play, the characters find themselves in hell and in their old traditional forms. Don Juan, as those will know who have seen Mozart's opera, was sent to hell for killing the father of Doña Ana, whom he seduced. The old father has come down from heaven, which is not the kind of place he understands or had expected. Ana has simply grown old and died and finds herself in hell for having been Juan's mistress.

It is not long, naturally, before the devil appears, recognizable as a minor character in the main play; and between them the four discuss heaven and hell and the truths of religion. This is all that really happens. The act resembles one of Plato's philosophical dialogues almost more than it does a dramatic performance. Nor does it really bear a close relation to the loves of Tanner and his Ann. Yet beautifully and persuasively presented with all the art of which Shaw is master are the central truths of the Shavian religion.

To Shaw, the power which shapes our universe is what he calls a Life Force. Starting from the dawn of our history, this Life Force has expressed itself through ever more complex forms of life, existing in and through them. Thus until it has evolved eyes, it cannot see. Until it has developed the mind of man, it is not able to contemplate itself or comprehend its own desires. It has been constantly trying to realize itself more perfectly, but it has only been able to proceed by trial and error. Thus the evils which we perceive around us in nature, such as pain, sickness, cruelty, and so forth, result from errors, or at least from experiments which are now outdated. So far, the Life Force has realized itself most perfectly in

Man; but it has not reached the end of its evolutionary process. Either Man must develop into Superman, as he himself has developed from anthropoid ancestors; or else he will be scrapped like the dinosaur and superseded by a better creation.

Such is Shaw's philosophy of life. It may seem barren to people who believe in a personal god, but there is no disputing the fact that it is the religion of an optimistic and an unselfish man. Says the Life Force to the philosopher: "I want to know myself and my destination, and choose my path; so I have made a special brain, a philosopher's brain — to grasp this knowledge for me, as the husbandman's hand grasps the plough for me. And this must thou strive to do for me until thou diest, when I will make another brain and another philosopher to carry on the work." In other words, the purpose of the philosopher is to be used, as the ploughman is used. He does not aspire to happiness, to immortality, or to any other reward. "This is the true joy in life," says Shaw in his preface to *Man and Superman*, "the being used for a purpose recognized by yourself as a mighty one; the being thoroughly worn out before you are thrown on the scrap heap; the being a force of Nature instead of a feverish selfish little clod of ailments and grievances, complaining that the world will not devote itself to making you happy."

Shaw is happy because he is being used for a great purpose; he is optimistic because he knows the world will grow better. Despite the failings of man, to which he is sensitive; despite the iniquities of the industrial system and the miseries of the poor, which are always on his conscience, he believes in a Life Force which continues to work. If Man is hopeless — and sometimes Shaw fears he is — then a more perfect creature must and will eventually develop. Human failure cannot divert the Life Force from its purpose.

For himself, Shaw asks nothing from the Life Force but the license to go on meddling.

> As long as I can conceive something better than myself, I cannot be easy unless I am striving to bring it into existence or clearing the way for it . . . It was the supremacy of this purpose that reduced . . . religion for me to a mere excuse for laziness, since it had set up a God which looked at the world and saw that it was good, against the instinct in me that looked through my eyes at the world and saw that it could be improved.

Thus confidently Shaw advanced against the whole of the nineteenth century, against its religion, its social organization, its morals, its learning. Fundamentally he did not think of himself as a playwright, but as a prophet whose bounden duty was to clear away the past in preparation for the future.

The remaining play in this great series, *Major Barbara*, is about religion, too; yet fundamentally it is the gospel of the social reformer. On many a Sunday when Shaw had stood up to speak in the open spaces of London, he had found himself next door to the Salvation Army, which also was speaking to the poor. In other words, though it held different beliefs, the Salvation Army had in some ways more in common with Shaw than he had with the professional groups which he loved to criticize for being the backbone of the established order. After his own meetings were over, therefore, Shaw would sometimes linger to talk to the Salvation Army lassies; and in gen-

Shaw addressing a working-class audience in London from the tailgate of a van.

eral he appreciated what the Army did for the poor of London.

Major Barbara is a conflict between two people who hate poverty. Barbara has joined the Salvation Army and is trying to teach people to rise above their deplorable conditions. Unfortunately in so doing, the Army helps to keep conditions as they are. The distillers and other such people who batten on the poor are perfectly ready to have the Army satisfy them, or even turn drifters into sober, industrious workmen. Thus Bodger the Brewer gives money to the Army, which takes it and blesses Bodger. Without him, the Army cannot keep its shelters open. Yet if he did not exist, shelters might not be needed. Barbara perceives that the Army, in spite of itself, has one standard for the rich and another for the poor.

Despairing of the Army for these reasons, Barbara turns to Undershaft, her father, a great armaments manufacturer. Undershaft is actually doing for nations what Bodger is doing for individuals, namely making money out of their passion for self-destruction. He does not apologize for this because to him money is all-important, however it is gained. Money is power, and Undershaft needs power to alter society. Poverty, he thinks, is the great sin, since poverty breeds ignorance, idleness, disease, and vice. Within the limitations of his vast, expanding business Undershaft already has abolished poverty; and he invites Barbara to save the souls of self-respecting men because they are worth saving.

This fascinating theme dominates a great play in

which Shaw's stature as an artist may clearly be seen. The vivid character drawing, the dramatic tension in the Salvation Army scene, the beautiful nature of Barbara, and the impressive abilities of Undershaft have always made this a favorite play. Notwithstanding, it presents a picture, too, of some of Shaw's foibles. He is too facile in argument, often more ready to shock than to convince. His own hatred of poverty is deeply felt; but the choice of an armaments manufacturer as hero is merely provocative. Impressive though Undershaft personally is, he rather gives us something to think of than proves a case. Nor does his argument agree with Shaw's opinions expressed elsewhere. This weakness in the play is further extended by a readiness to drop into farce for no reason. In *Man and Superman*, some events may be farcical; but we enjoy them as long as the argument is not so. In *Major Barbara*, the main events are a visit by Undershaft to Barbara's Army shelter, and of Barbara to Undershaft's factory town. There is nothing farcical about either; but Shaw's intelligence is too lively to put up with straight common sense. Thus he weakens the play at the end by a farcical argument which first proves Cusins, Barbara's fiancé, is a foundling and may be adopted as heir to the armaments business, and then goes on to state he has business ability on the basis of a piece of bargaining in which he does not know whether three-fifths is more than a half. This unreasonable carelessness in establishing Barbara's husband in the business not merely destroys the character of Cusins, but also makes the future success of Barbara so unlikely that one loses confidence. It is just this liveliness of unregulated fancy which at its best gives Shaw's work charm and at its worst persuades the reader that he has no opinions at all and is merely upsetting other people's for his amusement.

At about the same time that the seasons of the Court Theatre were introducing to a London public a greater playwright than England had produced for centuries, Shaw's reputation was spreading rapidly abroad. New York, as we have seen, led the way in the nineties with a successful run of *The Devil's Disciple.* A few years later Arnold Daley, a struggling young actor, read *Plays Pleasant* and *Plays Unpleasant,* which were widely and favorably reviewed in America. He conceived the idea of a series of matinees in New York after the fashion which started the run at the Court in London. Getting no response from managers and having three hundred and fifty dollars to invest, he engaged a cast and produced *Candida* himself in 1903. It made a great stir, and finally ran for a hundred and fifty performances, after which it went on tour. This encouraged Daley to put on *You Never Can Tell,* which ran for five months in 1905. In the same year, *Man and Superman,* though without the dream in hell, became the sensation of New York. Arnold Daley put on *Mrs. Warren* and was, as we have seen, arrested for it and released after a trial. He went on to play it in repertory, together with *Candida* and *John Bull.* Other companies went on tour with *Candida,* too; while theater groups put on performances in Philadelphia, Chicago and elsewhere. In England, Shaw never earned much money till 1911 with the run of *Fanny's First Play*, not one of his best. American audiences made him successful and rich at a time when in England he was merely admired by intelligent people who crowded short runs at the Court.

Meanwhile, his fame was spreading in Europe. In 1900 an Austrian named Trebitsch began translating his plays into German with the result that *Candida, The Devil's Disciple, Arms and the Man*, and *Cleopatra* all had successful runs in Berlin or Vienna between 1903 and 1905. The French, quite possibly because of their translator, were nearly ten years behind the times. In France, however, Shaw was discussed and read by intelligent people with appreciation of his worth. He was fifty in the year that *The Doctor's Dilemma* was produced at the Court, and after a long, slow start, he had at last arrived.

1912–1914

The Star of Stars

Lucinda Elizabeth Shaw died in 1913 at the age of eighty-three. When her son became prosperous, he made her an allowance, bought her a house, and urged her to take a box at the opera or have a car and chauffeur. Lucinda Elizabeth had refused such luxuries and gone on working till within a few years of her death. Music had never ceased to be a ruling passion; but as she grew older, spiritualism dominated her life. At first she had sought communication with Agnes, but later she also called poor George Carr Shaw from his lonely grave and made contact with Vandaleur Lee, whom in life she had abandoned. Finally she got in touch with a "Father John" whom she, a little senile at the end, described to her son as "a Cistercian monk who lived 6000 years before Christ."

With such contacts, Lucinda Elizabeth did not miss her son or greatly need him when he was out of sight. In his fame she took no interest. As far as he knew she had never even read "Corno di Bassetto," much less seen any of his plays. He did not resent this and indeed was grateful to his mother for the perfect independence she had allowed him and for her lack of possessive affection. It was Charlotte who never forgave her for her neglect of her son and did not visit her. After all, however, there was a well of tenderness in Lucinda Elizabeth, though buried deep. With incredulous surprise, Shaw found among her treasures the cap which he had worn as a baby. It gave him the feeling that he had never known her at all.

Shaw was head of his family by now. The foul-mouthed, exuberant Walter Gurley of his childhood had bought the goodwill of a medical practice in a country town outside London and settled there. Unluckily for him, the district rapidly developed into a lower-middle-class suburb, crammed with people who hardly ever summoned a doctor and could not pay him if they were forced to do so. Gurley could neither make a living nor afford to move, there being no goodwill left to sell. For years he was reduced to penury and used to borrow small sums from Lucinda Elizabeth. In 1899 he died, leaving to his nephew a gold watch, now for years in pawn, a few sticks of furniture, servants unpaid for ten years, and his father's Irish estate, encumbered with mortgages and poor relations. Shaw was forced to spend a good deal of money to put the place into repair; and now he found himself, in defiance of his principles, an absentee landlord.

Shaw's sister Lucy, despite her divorce, had for years devoted herself to her mother-in-law, who was a conventional suburban housewife with nothing in common either with Charlotte or Shaw. Lucy's relations with her

brother had always been cool ever since she had objected
to his arrival in London and had urged her mother to turn
him out of the house. But the very lack of affection which
pervaded the family life of the Shaws had prevented an
outright quarrel. Lucy felt neglected by Charlotte, who
did not like her. With her famous brother, she remained
on reasonable terms.

The theatrical event of the 1913 season was the Granville-Barker production of *Androcles and the Lion,* by far
the most original play which Shaw had published since
the great days of the Court Theatre six years earlier. In
form, *Androcles* is almost a pantomime, with a man in
lion's costume who dances a waltz with his rescuer. It is
typical of Shaw that he actually visited the zoo with the
actor playing his lion, in order to get the feel of the part.
Thus inspired, the lion was a roaring success, so that
The Times remarked: "of course it is the lion's evening.
Was ever a beast so fortunate? . . . we mean in being
the one character in the whole range of Shavian drama
who never talks."

Shaw said that he had written *Androcles* for children.
He admitted that the play was above their heads,
but stuck to it stoutly that *Androcles* was what children
really liked better than Barrie's *Peter Pan,* which was
only successful because it was what their parents thought
they enjoyed. He had to confess, however, that few children saw his play, which gave offense widely. In Berlin,
the German Crown Prince, head of a military clique, left
the theater when the Captain, clutching at his lost dignity in an argument with one of his prisoners, intoned:

"I call the attention of the female prisoner to the fact that Christians are not allowed to draw the Emperor's officers into arguments and put questions to them for which the military regulations provide no answer." In London, the *Daily Express* cried: "Christianity is scoffed at, martyrdom is lampooned, the beauty of faith is the subject of jeers." The *Church Times* called *Androcles* a "more direct affront to Christianity than any play of the past." To a generation brought up on dripping sentiment, it certainly appeared so.

The cause of the trouble was that Shaw's portrayal of early Christians displays his usual desire to talk about his own times. Thus his martyrs become recognizable types. Ferrovius, the hot-gospeler, has experienced salvation, but his new faith is at war with his bellicose instincts. Androcles, a mild, henpecked little man, will die for his principles but never fight for them. Spintho, a superstitious egotist, seeks his own advantage from religion, but has not the courage to be martyred, even in the hope of going to heaven. Lavinia, the only really noble character in the group, is not dying for a heavenly reward or because she thinks she knows all the truths of religion. She is going to the lions because she cannot compromise on vital issues. None of these people strikes pious attitudes like a saint in a picture.

Androcles has a charm and gaiety, but it is a serious discussion of the ways in which people face death and the things that they die for. The printed version has for its preface a long examination of the New Testament in which Shaw accepts the main teachings of Jesus, except those which claim that he is Son of God. What he rejects outright is the doctrine of the Atonement, an addition, as he points out, of St. Paul's. It outrages his sense of justice that anyone else should be punished for his sins or that God should accept this substitution. What is more remarkable perhaps than his conclusions is the amount of thought Shaw devotes to religion, his endless interest not only in his own faith, but in other people's. Some critics have gone so far as to say the religious temperament in varying aspects, good or bad, is the only one he deeply cares for.

While *Androcles and the Lion* was being presented to the public, Shaw had completed *Pygmalion*. He had a number of times written plays for special actors, including *The Devil's Disciple* for Richard Mansfield and *Captain Brassbound's Conversion* for Ellen Terry. Both these actors, however, were already interested in his work. With Mrs. Patrick Campbell, for whom he designed the part of Eliza, he had less connection.

Beatrice Stella Campbell, a dark beauty, half-English, half-Italian, had received the education of a lady, rather than of a professional actress. She had, however, made a runaway match with Patrick Campbell, who shortly proved unable to support her. The result was that after a few years he went to South Africa with the notion of sending for her as soon as he was established. Beatrice Stella was left with two children to support, and her husband's summons never came. She went on the stage and played in the provinces for small sums which she was glad to get until a lucky accident made her abilities

known, and she was chosen in 1893 for the leading role
in a play which set London talking. From that time forward she was one of the stars of the London stage, and
Shaw himself as drama critic wrote of her in ecstatic
terms.

> You will tell me, no doubt, that Mrs. Patrick
> Campbell cannot act. Who said she could? —
> Who wants her to act? — Who cares twopence
> whether she possesses that or any other second-
> rate accomplishment? On the highest plane one
> does not act, one *is*. Go and see her move, stand,
> speak, look, kneel — go and breathe the magic
> atmosphere that is created by the grace of all
> these deeds; and then talk to me about acting,
> forsooth!

He admitted her many faults when a role did not suit
her, yet thought that in her way she was incomparable.

As an actress and as a woman, Stella Campbell was
a complete contrast to her rival Ellen Terry. Stella was
all temperament and fury, notorious for her quarrels with
her leading men and her ability to wreck a scene which
did not happen to suit her. The insecurities of her early
life had taught her to use her claws freely. Even Ellen,
whose charity was almost universal, used to call her "Mrs.
Pat Cat" in her letters to Shaw. Although like all great
actresses, Stella had her courtiers, scandal had never
touched her; and although Campbell had died in 1901,
she had not remarried. People called her impossible to
live without—but impossible to live with.

Such was the actress whom Shaw for many years had

wished to use in a play. In 1897, when he had already begun *Caesar and Cleopatra*, he complained to Ellen Terry that it had been driven out of his head by a play he wanted to write for Forbes-Robertson and Mrs. Patrick Campbell, "in which he shall be a West End gentlemen and she an East End dona in an apron and three orange and red ostrich feathers." But in 1897, Stella Campbell was at the height of her glory and need not deign to consider the work of a playwright unless he was going to make money. By 1913, the cases were reversed. It was already twenty years since Stella had burst upon the scene, and she had not been quite a young girl then. Time was running out for her. On the other hand, since *Fanny's First Play* in 1911, Shaw had joined the ranks of the big money-makers. Whether for this reason or for some other, "that rapscallionly flower girl," as he had called her, was to have her part at last.

Charlotte wanted to go to Rome early in 1912, but Shaw resisted. This incessant travel was beginning to get on his nerves. He could only avoid accompanying her on the understanding that he would go abroad with her in August. His devotion to Charlotte was unshaken, but sometimes he thought it good for husbands and wives to have a vacation from each other.

To get Mrs. Patrick Campbell for his Eliza would be a difficult job. Stella might so easily fly off on a tangent or decide in her inimitable fashion to put the playwright in his place by showing how she despised him. She often did. Shaw brought a friend into the conspiracy, arranging to read the play to *her*. As if to surprise him, she would ask Mrs. Campbell to drop in. No slightest hint was to be given that there was a part involved. Just let her hear it!

Thus the matter was arranged. Stella sailed in, sharp claws hidden, but only prepared to listen with grace for a suitable moment to tear the play to shreds. Shaw started to read.

All went well through most of the first act until Eliza, startled by Professor Higgins, gives a howl: "A-ah-ah-ow-ow-ow-oo!"

"Oh please, Mr. Shaw, not that unpleasant noise: it's not nice!" minced Stella, taking advantage of a chance to spoil his effect.

Shaw read on unperturbed. About a page later, he produced the noise again.

"No, no, no, really, Mr. Shaw, you mustn't make that horrible sound. It's vulgar."

"Aaaaaaaaaaaaaaaaaah-ow-ooh! responded Shaw, louder than ever.

A conviction darted into Stella's mind that this flower girl was the chief part in the play. "You beast, you wrote this for me, every line of it," she burst out and settled herself to listen. At the end she rose to the occasion "quite fine and dignified for a necessary moment, and said unaffectedly that she was flattered." They agreed he should come to her house on the following day to discuss the casting.

Shaw went in triumph. This was going to be easy. When he came home again, however, he wrote to Ellen Terry: "And then — and then — Oh, Ellen, and then?

Why then I went calmly to her house to discuss business
with her, as hard as nails, and, as I am a living man, fell
head over ears in love with her in thirty seconds."

To Stella herself he protested more strongly: "when I
went into that room . . . I was a man of iron, insolently
confident in my impenetrability. Had I not seen you
dozens of times, and dissected you professionally as if
you were a microscopic specimen? What danger could
there possibly be for me? And in thirty seconds — oh,
Stella, if you had a rag of decency it *couldn't* have happened. I always thought that if I met you, I should ask
you to play. I looked at the piano; and I said, 'Good God!
Fancy listening to *that* when I can listen to her.' Is this
dignified? Is it sensible? at my age a driveller — a do-
tard! I will conquer this weakness or trade in it and write

The Star of Stars, Stella Campbell.

plays about it." For the moment, he decided to trade in it. The plays could come later.

Was he really in love with her? Can it be credible that a man of fifty-six, experienced in flirtation, should lose his heart to a woman in thirty seconds? It must be remembered that he liked to talk of love to ladies, particularly to actresses, who understood that his expressions meant less than they pretended. He had played this game with Ellen Terry under conditions which made it obvious that their relation was not definable in terms of love. He had wanted Ellen to act in his play. He had wanted Janet Achurch and had made love to her, too, in perfect confidence that her husband would understand there was nothing in it. Now he wanted the "Stella Stellarum," Star of Stars, and had perceived in a moment that she, too, enjoyed the game. He was launched at once on the wings of fancy. He adored her; and he had good reason to do so, since he had to persuade the most capricious lady in the theater to accept the leading man and the cast he wanted. But he did not like any mistake about his position either, and he warned her that he was an Irish liar who cared only for work, "treacherous as only an Irishman can be: he adores you with one eye and sees you with the other as a calculated utility."

There can be no reasonable doubt that the affair with Stella Campbell started in this fashion. The only question was, how long did he keep his head? This was no mere exchange of letters as with Ellen. They saw each other sometimes daily, and his Star of Stars was a woman of rare fascination. In six months, he was writing: "I

shall never quite get over . . . the falling in love. I
haven't been quite the same man since. Have you been
quite the same devil? For I suppose you *are* a devil: they
all tell me so when I go on raving about you."

Meanwhile, what happened to Stella's heart? Shaw's
beard and hair were whitening now, but Stella's looks,
still carefully preserved, could be relied on for a few more
years at least. Besides, she had other suitors, including
George Cornwallis West, brother of the Duchess of Westminster and second husband of Winston Churchill's
mother. Cornwallis West in his twenties had been considered the handsomest man in England. He was not
forty yet and younger than Stella, who guarded carefully
the secret of her age. It suited Stella well to have at her
feet England's most famous playwright, but was it to her
interest to fall in love with him? Thus Stella played the
game, but she too became a little overwhelmed. There
were those scenes between them — so many and so ten-
der. And his letters! "If I could write letters like you,"
she told him, swept right off her feet, "I would write letters to God."

Whatever the general public thought, or thinks to this
day, of the relation between the author and his star, there
was no doubt whatever what one particular person
thought. Charlotte was jealous.

Shaw had supposed she would have better sense. Why,
he never for an instant considered marrying his Stella
Stellarum! Whatever he felt for her, it had nothing to do
with his affection for Charlotte. They two had never pretended to be passionate lovers, but marriage had suited

them well. They were truly dear to each other. Why then should Charlotte have hysterics when he offered to someone else what she had never wanted?

Shaw had started by reading parts of his letters to Stella aloud to Charlotte, to persuade her that the whole thing was mere play-acting. Presently, however, he wrote to Stella that he was "snatching three lines to you and talking Insurance Act and the newspaper over my shoulder all the time, and then slipping the letter into my pocket lest anybody should see the address and be heartbroken." He had descended to secret telephone calls and assignations, even dragging his sister Lucy into the affair. He had no more dignity left than any clandestine lover, and he went through dreadful scenes with Charlotte. "It hurts me miserably to see anyone suffer like that. I must, it seems, murder myself or else murder her." It is a measure of the importance of the relationship that he pursued it.

They had genuine business together. Stella's suggestions for a leading man were quite impossible, and she quarreled violently with all of his. Nor were men anxious to act with her. "Go on for another play with Mrs. Campbell I will *not*," said one. "I'd rather die." *Pygmalion* was held up for a whole year, so that arrangements were made to bring it out first in Berlin and Vienna.

While negotiations dragged on, Stella for her part looked at the affair with disillusioned eyes. She was proud of her conquest, and Shaw's eloquence roused her to respond to his passion. Notwithstanding, all he offered her was a second-class position in his life. He never pretended that she took the place of Charlotte or that he aspired to marry her. Indeed, he annoyed her by his consideration in little matters, such as leaving her house in time to be punctual to Charlotte's meals. "Mr. Mouse can run so swiftly in and out of traps it's wonderful — but when Tabby mews — he trembles," she flashed at him.

An aging beauty who has never saved money needs to play her cards with care. All Stella was likely to get out of Shaw was the lead in a single hit whose earnings would run through her fingers as other earnings had done. When Ellen Terry had grown too old for leading parts, she had descended to asking for minor ones — and been refused. It would not do, Shaw said, to have the leading lady acted right off the stage. Would he grant to Stella what he had refused to Ellen, especially after his love cooled, as it surely would? Meanwhile, George Cornwallis West was offering marriage and could establish her in social circles which looked secure. For the moment, Stella engaged herself to Cornwallis West, but without interrupting her relationship with Shaw. If he could be married, why, so could she. About this time she started to call him "Joey the Clown," the circus artist who does not pretend to mean what he says or to look like his mask. But Joey's music was sweeter than the nightingale's, and she lingered to listen.

Early in 1913, the fifty-six-year-old Joey, who had learned to drive in 1908 and never drove well, bought a motor-bicycle in Coventry, got on it, and started out for Ayot some eighty miles off. "As I had never touched a motor-bicycle in my life, this might have ended in slaughter. Once coming suddenly on a vehicle round a corner and meaning to stop, I did the wrong thing and launched the machine forward like a thunderbolt. But there was a passage the size of a needle's eye and I shot through." He reached Ayot without any mishap but, a few yards from his gate, took a corner too fast, went into the bank, and fell off, though without much damage to the machine or himself. "I *can* ride a motor-bicycle," he recorded in triumph, "and now I would sell the machine for twopence. Men *are* fools, especially timid ones like me, always defying straws because the straws frighten them."

Joey's motor-bicycle had made him independent of Charlotte's car. His affair with Stella was coming to a climax, and he was actually prepared to create scandal. His insistence had brought her to the point of making a decision, too. She went to Brighton, and he followed. No doubt Stella knew by now that he could persuade her, even against her will. Pretending to be tired, she eluded him while she made arrangements. In the evening, she allowed him a little time, but put him off by talking of a long day tomorrow. She ordered refreshment; and the busboy who brought it said that since her bill was paid, she should settle in cash. She glanced at Joey, but he went on talking.

Next morning, he arrived at breakfast time and asked for his lady. They told him she had already left.

He poured out his feelings in letters, humiliated, reproachful, and hurt. If his sentiments toward her were not changed because she had treated him badly, he still made no effort to reestablish their relationship. She had told him once and for all that she wanted no more. She was still the Star of Stars and his Dark Lady, and he desired her to know how much he suffered.

Perhaps he saw this was no bad way to handle the matter, for Joey was nothing if not versatile. Rehearsals of *Pygmalion* were soon to commence. He would have to persuade his temperamental star to accept his criticism. Did he write her letters which flattered her ego with a purpose in mind?

If so, he made slight headway. Rehearsals were dreadful. Beerbohm Tree, who had been settled on at last for leading man, was a sentimental actor. Shaw went so far as to explain in a postscript to the printed play that Eliza did *not* marry Higgins, who was quite unsuitable for her. She married Freddy, who though weak and almost moronic, was ready enough to follow her lead. The two were established in a florist's shop and, after going to night school to learn how to keep accounts, made a success of it. This practical explanation would not do for Tree, who wanted to play Higgins with a romantic attachment to Eliza. Tree was an actor who thought a good deal of himself and was attended by a group of hangers-on who deferred to him. It offended him mortally when Shaw said in exasperation: "Must you be so *Treacly?*"

Tree's sulks were bad enough, but they were nothing to Stella's tantrums. She had always been an actress who exploited her own personality. Her methods did not appeal to Shaw, who told her she wanted too much limelight on her face and made it look like a dinner plate with two prunes on it. She did not take kindly to being told how she should deliver a line. No matter how he tried to flatter her, there was constraint between them. "I stamped my feet," she reminds him some years later, "and said in the voice of a Peacock: 'If Mr. Shaw does not leave the theatre I will' — With supreme dignity you gathered up your papers and left — without raising your hat to my valor."

After that he was reduced to writing notes of his corrections. She returned them unopened, and he — never to be outdone — enclosed them in a commercial envelope.

These difficult relations were made if anything worse by Mrs. Patrick Campbell's approaching marriage to George Cornwallis West. Shaw liked Cornwallis West, who was nobody's enemy unless perhaps his own; and he sincerely wished him luck in trying to live with Stella's temperament. All the same, the situation of a rejected suitor is awkward, and an edge of defiance was added to Stella's manner.

Needless to say, though she would not take trouble in rehearsals, Stella was wonderful when the day came. It was Shaw who had to destroy a series of photographs taken at this time which showed him looking "like an old dog who had been in a fight and got the worst of it." Green-eyed Charlotte, who had dignity of her own and had succeeded from time to time in being gracious, had found consolation in a spiritual discipline taught her by a certain Dr. Mills. In the company of Dr. Mills and his wife she had gone on her travels to the United States without attending the opening of *Pygmalion*. Relieved to find her "the happy consort of a happy man" once more, Shaw let her go.

Stella Campbell as Eliza Doolittle. London, 1914.

1900–1919

Heartbreak House

In 1898, marriage and illness had interrupted Shaw's political activity. He did not abandon it, however, or show himself less ready for hard work on the Fabian Executive or on the Borough Council of St. Pancras. Conventional members of the latter group, though delighted by his wit, were horrified by some of the causes he took up, including the indelicate one of providing public conveniences for the women of St. Pancras. Notwithstanding, his abilities made him a member of five of the most important committees of the Council; while in 1904, he actually stood for election as a delegate to the London County Council.

He had always been generous of time and effort in campaigning for other people, but had never stood for election before, since his seat on the Borough Council had been unopposed as the result of a political deal. To the dismay of his friends, his desire to educate the people of St. Pancras proved so much greater than his tact that they were forced to admit it would be useless to let him stand again. The chief issue in 1904 was the Education

Act, a landmark in British history, which, though passed a few years earlier, was still bitterly resented by nonconformists because it subsidized church schools as well as secular ones. To the fury of the Methodists in the borough, Shaw frankly told them church schools ought to be financed, in order to impose inspection and standardization. Teetotaler though he was, he then angered the temperance bloc by opposing local option in favor of municipal control. The circulars he sent out, ignoring party issues, appealed particularly to the large body of ratepayers who never troubled to vote. His utter defeat put an end to his chances for the future, while a change in the political climate of St. Pancras made it impossible for him to keep his seat there. The experience had lasted about long enough. It had given Shaw practical experience of how such bodies work; but it could never have become a major interest, especially after he began to succeed as a playwright.

The Fabian Society was a far more important part of his life. Marriage to a friend of the Webbs made his relationship with them more easy than it had been since Sidney's marriage. The first years of the twentieth century were the Fabian heyday. Beatrice and Sidney were the unofficial advisers of the Liberals, who were anxious to introduce reforms, a number of which had been suggested to them by Fabian tracts. At the same time, however, the increasing eminence of both Shaw and the Webbs created a division between them and the rest of the society. Shaw's plays and the Webbs' monumental books were manifestations of individual genius, not Fa-

bian work. To complicate matters, the foundation of the
Labour Party in 1906 put the Fabians in an awkward
position. They supported it, of course; but it was with the
Liberals that their strength lay, so that they were reduced
to running with the hare and hunting with the hounds,
which did not please either.

For all these reasons, the Fabian Society went through
a serious crisis early in the century. It must be remembered that, though founded twenty years before, it still
had the same group of leaders with the methods and
purpose that they had imposed in the beginning. The
Fabian Society was small, and it operated on a shoestring.
Deliberately the leaders had not made it easy to join. One
had to attend meetings, be recommended by two members of the group, and finally submit to a year's probation
and demonstrate willingness to work. Most of the people
who got through this screening process were very able
and had ideas of their own. Many of them had political
ambitions which led them later to the upper echelons of
the Labour Party. It by no means followed that an organization which suited the Webbs, who were backstairs politicians, or Shaw, who was no politician at all, would seem
perfect to a younger generation.

The first step in what became a famous quarrel was
taken when the Fabian Society elected H. G. Wells in
1903. The political novels of Wells are almost forgotten
today, while his science fiction has been superseded by
cruder stuff which is more up-to-date. When he was writing, however, about the issues of his own time, Wells had
tremendous vitality. Great fame came to him easily, and

those who trouble to read him today can perceive it was not undeserved.

In background Wells was a new man, not sprung like Shaw from down-at-heels gentlefolk, but from the servant class. His mother was housekeeper to a great house with forty servants, and his father was a professional cricketer kept on the estate. Wells was a little man of unimposing presence with a squeaky voice; and either for this reason or because he had been too much patronized as a child, he had a great capacity for taking offense. He was incapable of opposing anyone on grounds of principle without developing a personal quarrel. Notwithstanding these drawbacks, however, he was a genuine liberal, fertile in excellent ideas and devoted to valuable causes. Wells was welcomed by the Fabians with open arms, and presently he began to express his own ideas about their future.

Early in 1906, Wells read a paper called "The Faults of the Fabian" to the society, in which he called for a thorough transformation. The Fabian was niggling and needlessly poor. Its backstairs influence was smaller than it supposed; yet it had no other and could not have under its present constitution. The time had come to expand, hire ample quarters, pay office workers, and campaign for a larger membership. What the country needed was a dedicated group of the politically conscious, self-elected as it were, to guide and handle the ignorant and indifferent mass of voters. Wells was asking for something comparable to the party system under dictatorship. The Nazi, Communist, and Fascist parties of the twenties and thirties were composed, not of the nation, but of people who wanted to join and gave the lead. Such comparisons need not suggest that Wells was communist or fascist. It was merely that, thinking over the practical difficulties of government by democracy, he had come up with a notion which was of sufficient value to be adapted later by other critics of their times, both Right and Left. Now he called for a committee to draw up proposals for making the Fabians into an active political group with this in mind.

This would be a transformation indeed for the Fabian! Wells was aware that opposition from the Old Gang would be automatic. It being his habit to make his quarrels personal, he did not hesitate to deliver an attack on the "foolish laughter" which pervaded Fabian meetings. The cause, as he need hardly explain, was Mr. Shaw. That gentleman, he freely admitted, was serious-minded.

> You will not (I hope) suppose that . . . I am assailing Bernard Shaw. But I do assail the strained attempts to play up to Shaw, the constant endeavors of members devoid of any natural wit or wildness to catch his manner, to ape his egotism, to fall in with an assumed pretence that this grave high business of Socialism is an idiotic middle-class joke.

This perhaps was decently disguised, if embarrassing within the Fabian family. As the dispute progressed, Wells threw discretion to the winds and denounced the Old Gang as liars, tricksters, and reactionaries in terms that are more familiar in communist circles than they ever became in Fabian ones.

Sidney Webb, who was chiefly attacked, made no answer. His temper was unruffled and, though unrivaled in committee meetings, he was not this kind of controversialist. When the matter came to a final vote in a tense meeting, Wells was entrusted to Shaw, who without perceptible effort made mincemeat of him.

The two were unevenly matched. Wells, so persuasive with his pen, was a miserable speaker, squeaky, inaudible, glued to his manuscript. He hardly came up to Shaw's shoulder, and his appearance was in every way unimpressive. His unfortunate combination of personal abuse with genuine plans, allowed Shaw to point out that the characters of himself, the Webbs, and their other colleagues were called in question. Therefore, if a single individual voted with Wells, the Old Gang would resign in a body and found another group. Leaving this terrific threat to sink in, he descended, as Wells had done, to the personal level, but with far greater skill.

Mr. Wells had complained of the long delay of the Old Gang in replying to his report. "But we took no longer than he. During his committee's deliberations, he produced a book on America. And a very good book, too. But whilst I was drafting our reply, I produced a play." Shaw paused and let his eyes drift around the ceiling till his audience, embarrassed, thought he had lost the drift of what he was going to say. Not until the situation had really become strained did he resume. "Ladies and gentlemen, I paused to enable Mr. Wells to say, 'And a very good play too.'"

The audience burst into laughter, while Wells on the

platform smiled self-consciously. Delighted at the sudden release from a tension in which they all had been gripped, people rolled about until they were too exhausted to laugh any longer. Wells, who was not a fool, withdrew his amendment, rather than find himself unsupported. The matter was closed.

The Fabian went on as before, but the Old Gang had seen the handwriting on the wall. Presently it would be best for them to get off the executive committee, leaving the work to be done by younger men. They took their time about it, but in 1911 the thing was accomplished. The Webbs devoted themselves to a new offshoot, the New Fabian Research Bureau. In 1911, Sidney founded *The New Statesman,* a political weekly which has already passed its fiftieth year. As for Shaw, he no doubt rejoiced in having more time for other business. He subscribed, however, half the modest sum which was needed to get *The New Statesman* going, and he promised articles. These he refused to sign, as a method of preserving his right to say whatever he pleased. The editor, who might not have dared to cut his contributions if they had been signed, offended him by displaying no scruples when they were not. *The New Statesman,* and the Fabian Society itself, saw little of Shaw after this time, though he attended the Fabian Summer School for years, life and soul of the party, and delivered the concluding lecture in a series which the Fabian Society arranged in London, right up to their fiftieth anniversary in the mid-thirties. Substantially, however, Shaw's work for the Fabian was done. Socialism and an interest in politics remained.

They were to find expression increasingly in his plays from this time forward.

By 1911, as he retired from the Fabian Executive, Shaw was growing famous and rich. The money made little difference to his manner of life. His socialist principles did not suggest that it was possible to live as one ought under capitalism. Thus he did not give his money to the poor, since private charity could not in his view reform an iniquitous system. Though on occasion generous, he was of a saving disposition in reaction to the insecurities of his youth. The Shaws lived comfortably because Charlotte wished to do so, but they had no expensive tastes in house or furnishings. They traveled first class and stayed in the best hotels, but the list which Charlotte presented everywhere as "Mr. Shaw's Diet" suggested the simplest dishes instead of meat, such as macaroni and cheese, dry white beans boiled, or curried rice. His clothes, still mildly eccentric, were bought for utility and worn until they became disreputable, when Charlotte saw to it they were disposed of.

Money did little for Shaw except to allow him to be excellently taken care of, to travel about, and to pursue his active life without considering its incidental costs. Fame, on the other hand, made great demands. The business of a prophet is to preach in season and out of season. He is always on duty. Accordingly, Shaw studied his public behavior in the same deliberate fashion that he had earlier studied public speaking. Since people expected him to be brilliant when they met him, he laid himself out to be entertaining, thus keeping the conversation on his

own terms. Since interest in the private life of a famous
man is endless, he tried to anticipate curiosity by reminisc-
ing freely. He even chose an official biographer, an
American professor, thus fending off people who could
have kept running over for weekends and been a nuisance.

His interest in himself was open and endless. In intro-
verted people, this state of mind is taken for granted.
When it happens to a man who gives the impression of
being a complete extrovert, as Shaw had taught himself
to do, it is generally described as vanity. Those who
called Shaw vain did not perceive that the process by
which he spun his thoughts into plays was only possible
through constant self-analysis. In every play at least one
character is bound to think like Shaw and voice opinions
which he either holds or considers plausible. Quite fre-
quently bits and pieces of him are scattered through a
number of people, in order that the battle of ideas may
be fought out on equal terms. Thus Shaw was bound to
be conscious of himself; and he deliberately displayed this
state of mind without inhibition.

He loved to be photographed and was always interested and critical of the result. He liked to sit for his portrait. In 1906 Charlotte decided that she wanted a really
good memorial of him. He replied that he would sit for a
bust for Rodin, the most famous sculptor of the day, who,
being a Frenchman and not interested in the drama, had
never heard of him. Charlotte sent Rodin a thousand
pounds, not in payment for a work which he might not
wish to do, but in general contribution to his art. Thus

flattered, the sculptor could hardly refuse to take some interest in the project; and he asked if Shaw would sit for him in Paris. Charlotte and her husband set off at once and were there next morning. Shaw was perfectly ready to devote a month to the sittings and ever after liked to display the result. The Rodin bust was followed by four other busts by well-known sculptors, three of which found home with the Shaws, together with photographs, caricatures, sketches, and portraits, until the Shavian beard in various guises bristled all over the drawing room at Ayot as well as the London flat.

Such developments were really little more than the peculiar setting which Shaw created for his public sayings. Increasingly, after he gave up the Fabian, he spoke for himself on public issues; and he wanted to be heard by a vast audience. In this he was supremely successful,

Bust of Shaw by the famous French sculptor Auguste Rodin.

though it is difficult to tell whether the annoyance which he deliberately aroused had the effect which he desired. Certainly his sayings stuck in the mind and were often perceived to have been sensible twenty years later when the controversy which had provoked them was perfectly dead. On the other hand, a reputation for flippancy prevented his being listened to, even on occasions where he might have had a good effect. As a dramatist, he had an enormous influence on his generation, but as a politician, after he left the Fabian, very little.

It is a measure of the solidity of the nineteenth-century world that the Fabian Society could concern itself purely with the state of England and have no foreign policy to speak of. In the Boer War it was hopelessly divided. Some were pacifists, and others, including the Webbs and Shaw, took the view that socialism required an industrial civilization. For this reason, the rule of the British must be preferable to the backward, rural, bigoted state of the Boers, which could lead nowhere. This rather unscrupulous view resulted from lack of reflection and the coolness of the Fabian mind, which was impervious to the heats of nationalism, be they Boer or British. Thus when the nationalistic fervors of Germany and France began to raise the temperature of Europe in the early 1900's, Fabians, and Shaw in particular, were unsympathetic. Mass emotion always has a hysterical side, and Shaw detested it. He lost no opportunity of trying to puncture it with a sharp word.

In 1912, he made himself unpopular by speaking out about the loss of the *Titanic*, a luxury liner which struck an iceberg and went down on its maiden voyage. There were not enough lifeboats, and the loss of life was great. Newspapers made tremendous stories out of people crying "Women and children first" and giving up their seats to others, of wives who refused to be saved without their husbands, and of doomed passengers singing "Abide with me" as the ship went down. It was left to Shaw to point out in a public letter that the ship had been lost by the grossest carelessness, that the lack of boats was a scandal, and that, despite the gallantry of some, sailors and passengers had by no means all displayed that stiff upper lip and gentlemanly conduct which the papers were calling traditional British virtues. He was perfectly right, and the sentiment displayed over the *Titanic* was in poor taste. Nevertheless, this was an example of the prophet speaking out of season. Like a terrier, Shaw barked whenever anything annoyed him. By the time that World War I commenced, the general public had already learned to discount what he said.

The shadow of World War I had darkened Europe for ten years before it broke out. In particular, since the crisis of Agadir in 1911, every nation of importance was preparing for the future in a spirit of pure self-interest. None could afford to be taken unprepared, so that all were arming. The situation was one which every sensible man deplored, and yet nobody had a constructive answer. Of all intelligent men Shaw was least qualified to deal with a problem which involved emotions which he distrusted and a worldwide climate characteristic of a new century which had opened when he was already over forty. Only the urgency of the situation can excuse him for pressing solutions which revealed his ignorance.

England, France, and Germany, cried Shaw, should form a league, agreeing that any two of them — or even all three — would combine against the aggressor. In this blithe fashion he ignored the tendencies of modern diplomacy, the way in which Bismarck by a skillful forgery had fastened on France in 1870 the guilt of beginning a war which he was determined to have. He had failed to anticipate the ingenuity of Hitler, who started World War II by an "invasion" of German territory by fake Polish troops who withdrew, leaving behind them corpses of concentration camp prisoners dressed in Polish uniforms. He had even ignored the facts of logistics which compelled the French to order mobilization a few days before the Germans because their railroad system had been less carefully developed for war, so that their forces took longer to collect. Less at home in the political sphere than he was in the economic, Shaw lost prestige by treating the issues as simple.

Nothing that Shaw could have said would have prevented World War I, but he had put himself in a bad position to offer advice by the time it arrived. Nor could he keep silent during the struggle, merely because he had nothing positive to say. Thus when the end of the war came, and he might have encouraged a constructive policy, he had no influence.

Though it sometimes seemed hard to believe, Shaw really supported a war to the bitter end against German militarism. Germany, however, was not and never had been his business, which was to call England to repentance. World War I put an end for about four years to serious drama, as actors and audiences were swept into the army. Entertainments were of the music hall type popular with troops on leave. England was simply not in the mood for what Shaw called "the terrible castigation of comedy." Shaw did not even try to write a serious play, though it might probably have been performed in New York. He had nothing to say to New York, and he was not in comedy spirits, particularly as the never-ending slaughter went on in Flanders, almost in sight of the British coast, and sometimes in hearing. Nevertheless, he could not stand by in helpless silence while terrible things went on. The consequence was, he put his thoughts together in a pamphlet entitled *Commonsense about the War*, which *The New Statesman* had the temerity to publish.

It was fortunate for Shaw that nineteenth-century England had been unusually tolerant and that its traditions were not quite dead. *Commonsense about the War* is more concerned with exploding hysteria about gallant Belgium and Britain's honor than it is to encourage the troops. He admits that "as I had practically adopted England by thrusting myself and my opinions on her in the face of every possible rebuff, it was for me to take the consequences, which certainly included an obligation to help my reluctant ward in her extremity, as far as my means allowed." This handsome acknowledgment did not alter the fact that parts of *Commonsense about the War* were used by the enemy as propaganda, or that

Shaw's comparison of Edward Grey, the British foreign minister, to a German Junker was manifestly unfair. Tilting against the things he most disliked, hysteria, and indeed the war itself, he did not reflect that the only great nation to face the war without conscription was actually dependent on the feelings he deplored. *Commonsense about the War* reads well today when we are not fighting for our lives. Its tone is sensible, and the exaggerations which Shaw uses to drive home his points do not distress us. At the time it raised a tremendous outcry. People cut Shaw or refused to be seen in his company. His mailbox was crammed with abusive letters, many of which were so unpleasant that Shaw, who employed a woman secretary, published a request that such correspondents should write the word "obscene" on the top left-hand corners of their envelopes.

This feeling had hardly died down before the sinking of the *Lusitania* aroused the public to fresh transports of rage against the Germans. Yet why should the drowning of a few saloon passengers be so important compared to the slaughter of the nation's young men? Shaw spoke out in this sense and roused another tempest, in the midst of which he resigned from the Dramatists' Club as an alternative to expulsion.

Despite Shaw's tendency to anger everyone, the British government was anxious to use his talents and prestige in propaganda; and he himself was willing that they should. He was accordingly taken over to Flanders and shown around, an experience which he could not help enjoying, despite its horror. Displaying his usual good sense, he offered to drive himself across the market square of Ypres, which was being shelled, on the grounds that it would be a waste of serving soldiers if they were killed while driving about a mere civilian. This experience, however, produced no great result. Three playlets which he did write on war themes were none of them precisely what the propagandists wanted.

O'Flaherty, V.C. is about an Irish boy who went to war for the excitement of it, won the Victoria Cross, and has returned a man. It soon appears that he has grown out of his enthusiasm for war, having learned to look on the enemy soldier as a decent lad like himself. On getting back to Ireland, he finds he has grown out of his country as well. The provincial ignorance and peasant greed, the narrow view, the pettiness of the continual quarrel with England all revolt him. The end of it is, he says he is going to marry in France and settle down in a civilized country. Shaw averred that *O'Flaherty, V.C.* was intended to encourage Irish recruitment. Authorities who knew more about the subject decided that it would have the reverse effect.

Augustus Does His Bit is a silly little play, satirizing the stupid fool of a gentleman-subaltern in a cushy job at home. Augustus was too easy game for Shaw, who might have left him to more obvious minds. Perhaps it was merely that in the prevailing emotional climate, it was hopeless for even Shaw to keep his head.

The Inca of Perusalem, which dares to make fun of the Kaiser, strikes perhaps the most effective note, though it was not well received. "Many were so horribly afraid of

him that they could not forgive me for not being afraid of
him: I seemed to be trifling heartlessly with a deadly
peril." Actually Shaw's portrait of the Kaiser, though
broadly comic, comes closer to the real character of the
man than did public opinion, which conceived of him as
a universal bogey. In a subdued fashion, Shaw was putting in another plea for sense, once more disregarded.

During the war, Shaw was at least in favor of fighting
until it was won. As victory actually loomed in sight, he
was out of sympathy with the general tendencies of British policy. For the peace terms, the postwar blockade,
the "Hang-the-Kaiser" movement, and other excesses
of the victorious side he had no good word. Wilson's
Fourteen Points appealed to him by their moderation;
but by not holding his tongue on earlier occasions, he had
lost his chance of speaking with authority now. This did
not prevent him, of course, from publishing *Peace Confer-
ence Hints*, containing the suggestion that a league of
great powers with well-developed labor and socialist
movements would be far more effective than a general
League of Nations.

His hints were not taken and hardly seriously discussed. The earlier optimism with which Fabians had
faced the task of converting the British government to
socialism was giving way to a feeling of hopeless aliena-
tion. England did not go socialist in 1918; she merely
gave votes to women, thereby doubling the numbers of
the ignorant who were able to make their appalling judgments count in government. Internal problems, which the
Fabians had expected to solve by gradual progress, were

now compounded by international ones which England
mismanaged as badly as she had always mismanaged Ireland. To these even Fabians had not worked out solutions.

Already in 1913, Shaw had started work on a play
which he intended as an indictment of the leadership of
England in the years preceding World War I. At intervals during the war he had worked on it, and in 1918 in
the disillusion of victory he completed it at last. To many
people *Heartbreak House* is Shaw's subtlest work. In the
manner of Chekhov in *The Cherry Orchard,* it expresses
what it has to say by bringing together a group of people
who at first sight have nothing to do with the real subject.

Captain Shotover, senile now, drunken, a little crazy,
has built his house like the ship he used to command. But
his ship drifts masterless now that he is old, though he still
remembers what leadership is in his lucid moments. "Let
a man drink ten barrels of rum a day, he is not a drunken
skipper until he is a drifting skipper. Whilst he can lay his
course and stand on his bridge and steer it, he is no drunkard. It is the man who lies drinking in his bunk and trusts
to Providence that I call the drunken skipper, though he
drank nothing but the waters of the River Jordan."

Captain Shotover's house, his ship, is England. His
son-in-law asks him: "And this ship we are all in? This
soul's prison we call England . . . what am I to do?"

"Learn your business as an Englishman," is the answer.
"Navigation. Learn it and live; or leave it and be
damned."

No one, however, perceived the truth of the captain's

saying, except perhaps one young girl who is too inexperienced to take command. Captain Shotover's daughters, their husbands, lovers, or guests are all too busy analyzing themselves and their emotions. They are all divorced from reality. The millionaire does not really own his own millions; the brave man prefers romances to his real achievements. Even the beauty of the ladies is half sham. "A good deal of my hair is quite genuine," admits one frankly. As for the would-be reformer in the group, he has discovered that nothing ever does really get reformed.

Something happens at last in the shape of an air raid. Death and danger at least are immediate sensations. As the youth of England rushed forth to die in 1914, so the inhabitants of Heartbreak House tear down the curtains and light up every room in frantic excitement. But the zeppelin goes by, its only victims being those who have fled the house to a place of safety.

"Safe!" says the girl disappointedly.

"Yes, safe," agrees another. "And how damnably dull the world has become again suddenly." Captain Shotover's daughter Hesione has the last word:

"What a glorious experience! I hope they'll come again tomorrow night."

They all hope so. War is actually a relief from the eternal discussions which get nowhere and the emotions in which all are wallowing for want of anything worthwhile to do. Shaw has pictured in *Heartbreak House* the ruling intelligentsia of England. Beside it, he has roughly sketched in as a contrast Horseback Hall, home of the hunting, shooting aristocracy. As we may suppose, Horseback Hall has no advice of any value; nor would it matter if it had, since Heartbreak House would only use it to start another discussion.

Heartbreak House as a work of art stands among Shaw's great plays, even though it will never be his most popular one. As a political tract, it has the disadvantage of being partly out-of-date when it was published. The small, tight circle of the political ruling class, in which everybody knew everybody else, was broken up in World War I. It continued to exist in shadow, but as an enemy it was not worth fighting against. Its days were numbered. What did persist was the lack of leadership about which Shaw complained, but for this *Heartbreak House* devised no remedy.

By 1919 when *Heartbreak House* was first performed, it had become obvious that the fresh look at social and moral standards for which Shaw had been pleading since the eighties was actually being taken. World War I had brought this about, but the influence of Shaw on it was tremendous. Politically, however, he was still ineffective. The leadership of England in the twenties and thirties can never be compared for an instant to the prewar Liberal government which combined the formidable intellect of Asquith with the brilliance of Lloyd George and the energies of Churchill. It was one thing to call for leadership, another to produce it.

1919–1925

Methuselah and Joan

SHAW WAS sixty-three in 1919 and his hair and beard were white, but he did not feel old. Every morning that he was in town he walked at his usual headlong pace down Pall Mall to swim in the pool of the Royal Automobile Club before breakfast. Punctually at ten he sat down to work in his study, composing his plays in the same small room as his secretary, who was kept busy transcribing the neat shorthand of the day before or sorting his ever-increasing mail. Shaw never actually worked at his current play much more than four hours in a day, but Sundays and holidays were all alike to him. He usually went down to Ayot for long weekends, leaving his secretary behind; but mail deliveries in England were speedy, so that each day's composition was ready on her desk the following morning.

Shaw never revised his work until it had been typed, and compared to most creative writers he wrote with speed. Though he was not careless with words, they came to him rapidly. A perfectionist above all, he spent endless time on detail, fussing about every punctuation mark and often calling on Charlotte to help in his terrible struggle over proof. Indeed, it was not the actual dialogue which took so long as the stage directions, not merely the entrances and exits, but the movements of characters about the stage or the arrangement of necessary furniture on it.

Even so, Shaw's working hours far more than covered the time he actually spent on his great dramas. Minor works poured out of him: parodies of Shakespeare, farces, curtain-raisers for special occasions, letters to the papers about literary or political matters which chanced to be topical, articles or speeches, trivialities like a motoring guide to the Scottish Highlands which he sent to the Royal Automobile Club with his frank opinion of the places he had seen and their hotels, conscientiously including information of no interest to himself, such as where they served liquor. If all else failed, he gave advice, composing for instance an excellent small pamphlet which he reproduced at his own expense and sent out to aspiring authors who wrote and asked him how to get their plays performed.

Not infrequently when he was in London, working time was cut into by interviews. Many people wanted to meet him, and yet he seldom went out socially. It was not that he paraded his diet, but that the sociability produced by large meat meals and plenty of liquor simply bored him. People visited Ayot or were invited to lunch at the London flat; but Shaw felt obliged to be brilliant for guests, so that he generally preferred a meal with Charlotte in companionable silence.

Throughout the twenties and thirties he was still active on committees. He was, for instance, on the council of the Royal Academy of Dramatic Art and always recommended to young people who wanted to go on the stage that they should enroll there. For years he presided over dress rehearsals of student performances, working as hard to give them polish as he ever had done on professional rehearsals.

Vigorous as he still was, it could hardly be supposed that he had run out of things to say, or even that he had spent the years of World War I putting touches to *Heartbreak House* and writing the minor plays or pamphlets which were all that he actually published. In fact, he was making a tremendous effort to rise to a great concept and to give a world which desperately needed one a positive message.

Back to Methuselah, which he finished at last in 1920, is not just a play. In fact, it is five plays of varying lengths, making altogether an epic two-and-one-half times the length of *Saint Joan*. Its purpose was to give back to mankind a sense of religious values by developing what amounts to a parable, a story not of what did or what will happen, but of the direction in which Shaw felt mankind should be going. Not since Milton opened *Paradise Lost* by expressing his intention to "justify the ways of God to man" has any English author aspired to such a grand achievement. In the event, Shaw failed less gloriously than Milton; yet if *Back to Methuselah* swept very few off their feet, it deserves recognition as a work on a remarkable scale in which Shaw attempted to sum up his ideas on ultimate value.

In *Man and Superman* Shaw had already outlined a religion in which the Life Force seeks to incarnate itself in living creatures which evolve as a result of its inner drive. Man, as we have seen, must become superman by taking some step which in the earlier play is obscure. In *Back to Methuselah*, for the sake of demonstrating his meaning, Shaw pretends that the step taken is going to be that of living longer. As matters are, people start to

The Old Rectory, Ayot St. Lawrence.

get old just about as life has taught them a few things. Besides, they often commit themselves to follies, as they would never do if they had the expectation of living to face the consequences of them. Now it matters not at all whether living longer would actually make people better and wiser. *Back to Methuselah* assumes it will, merely for the purpose of showing what "better" and "wiser" are in human terms.

Shaw starts with an introductory play in which he establishes the relation of his theme to the whole history of mankind by a beautifully poetic account of Adam and Eve, showing how the impulse to achieve perfection has been present from the beginning. Having thus set the mood of the whole, he skips immediately to present times and does not hesitate to make this clear as day by introducing Lloyd George and Asquith, the rival leaders of the Liberal Party, who both attempt to gain political support by claims and promises which they cannot possibly back up. The real theme of the play, however, is the assertion by a distinguished biologist and his brother that the moment for the great transformation is at hand, and that a few people are going to live for three hundred years instead of dying.

In the third play this turns out to have happened to a curate and a parlormaid who both appeared briefly in the second. Their wisdom is now so great that they are respectively Archbishop of York and a Cabinet Minister. Unfortunately the rest of the politicians have not improved, so that the Longlivers realize they are going to become a race apart.

We next skip a thousand years and find that this has
happened. The Longlivers have taken over Ireland
(empty, of course, because its original inhabitants could
not wait to get out of the island). To make use of their
wisdom come the politicians with their usual stupid questions about which of them is going to win the game which
they are still playing. By now the Longlivers are so wise
they have all sorts of mysterious powers and are so intoler-
ant of the wicked stupidity of the rest that they consider
putting an end to them. Indeed, it is clearly shown that
the two races cannot exist together any more. An Elderly
Gentleman who is one of the Shortlivers, but who has always attempted within his limitations to face truth, is so
disillusioned when he sees his fellows as they are that
he refuses to go back home with them. In vain the Long-
liver informs him that he cannot so much as look on her
unveiled. He insists that he will do it, and falls dead.

Finally in the fifth play the great millennium has arrived. Man is perfect at last and more or less immortal.
But what is he? A disembodied thought, contemplating
in ecstasy what appears to be pure mathematics. To be
sure a man is still born and still goes through the stages
which at present make up our life. But the process of
evolution has telescoped these, so that the human being is
incubated until about seventeen and then, being born,
goes through the pleasures of love and creative art in four
years of adolescence. By the end of that time he is already unable to enjoy any pleasures but thought. Eventually thought gives him so much power over his body that
he dispenses with it and goes on thinking without it.

It is this barren result in which all the noble and excellent things in our lives except mathematics are ruth-
lessly swept away that kills *Back to Methuselah*. For all
the dignity to which it sometimes attains, we are not impressed. Shaw may inform us that the pleasure of pure
thought is many times greater than all other pleasures
combined. We do not believe him. His suggestion that
we must outgrow art and love does not convince us. Despite its failure, however, this cycle of plays has a great
dignity and at least one poignant moment when the Elderly Gentleman, who was made up in New York as Shaw
in person, falls dead because he cannot bear the face of
truth.

It seemed improbable that Shaw would ever be able to
see this vast creation on the stage. That he did so was due
to Barry Jackson, a producer of genius who had started
out with an amateur company playing one night a week
in Birmingham. Five years later, his enthusiasm had
raised the money for a Birmingham Repertory Theatre
which proceeded to make itself a national reputation.
Shaw went up there in person to see a matinee of *Heartbreak House* and was naturally escorted by Barry Jackson,
who took the chance to ask him for permission to produce
Back to Methuselah, which had hitherto been attempted
only by the Theater Guild in New York. In answer, Shaw
inquired skeptically whether Jackson's wife and family
were provided for — as otherwise they would certainly
end in the poorhouse. Reassured on this point, he gave
his permission and promised to attend the last rehearsals.

It took Barry Jackson nearly two months of hard work

to get the enormous play ready for production. It had to be divided into parts, played on four successive nights. Shaw meanwhile, traveling as usual with Charlotte, had gone to Ireland. While he was scrambling about on some rocks, he slipped and fell heavily on his back, driving the camera which he carried slung from his shoulder into his side. He cracked several ribs, and though the Irish doctors strapped him up, he arrived at Birmingham in great pain, almost unable to move. Luckily Birmingham had a famous osteopath who, after a long struggle, succeeded in setting Shaw to rights. Undeterred by the muscular soreness which must have followed, Shaw worked through all the dress rehearsals, attended the performances, and witnessed the visible emotion of the audience which, stunned by the vastness of the great conception, was at first unable to cheer the last performance.

This was a high point of his life. Shaw very seldom appeared to a call of "author!" but on this occasion he not only did so but made a short speech. What was more, as soon as the curtain fell, the astonished cast beheld him execute an impromptu dance on the stage, entirely forgetful of the injuries which had almost prevented his moving ten days before. Presently *Back to Methuselah* transferred for a short season to the Court Theatre in London. Barry Jackson had won Shaw's lasting gratitude, as he was to discover.

While *Back to Methuselah* was going into production, Shaw was at work on a masterpiece of a different sort. He had always wanted to write a drama about a great religious figure, and Mahomet was his first choice. Even he, however, could perceive that a Shavian version of Mahomet on the public stage could cause an international incident. Turkey and the Arab countries, some of which were in British hands since the war, would be mortally offended. Indeed, it was likely that such a play would be censored and never reach production. Reluctantly, after having long cherished the project, Shaw abandoned Mahomet.

Charlotte was certain that Joan of Arc was a better subject. In 1913, they had visited Joan's home town of Domrémy, and Shaw had been inspired to read the accounts of her trial. They had given him the thought that Joan was an early Protestant because she steadfastly held to her personal experience, and defied the authority of the Church. The concept interested him, but for many years it lay unused. He turned once more in this direction partly because he had revised his ideas of human greatness since the days when he idolized Napoleon and Caesar. Napoleon had actually figured in *Back to Methuselah* as an example of the folly and wickedness of man. Shaw was looking for a figure which could express more nearly his aspirations.

He brooded over the problem while Charlotte cunningly strewed books on Joan of Arc about the house. Presently her tact and knowledge of him prevailed, and he began.

Among the plays of Shaw, *Saint Joan* is the general favorite. Everything harmonizes in it to produce a splendid whole. Charlotte's choice of heroine, for instance, justifies itself. Joan's aspirations are lofty, but they are not complicated, so that the thinking in the play is all of it Shaw's. This leaves Joan free to perform her task of lifting ordinary people out of themselves without engaging in complex argument. Her simple inspiration can be contrasted with the reasoning of her adversaries, whose different methods of approach serve to remind us of the trouble the world always has with saints, one way or another. *Saint Joan* as a result has a universal application which raises it above its natural rival, *Caesar and Cleopatra*.

In developing this fine theme, Shaw has been able to restrain his natural exuberance. Nothing, for instance, is more conspicuous in his plays than his power of character drawing, but this develops only too often into caricature. Similarly his humor, which lightens every play, becomes too readily farce. Both elements are present in *Saint Joan*. De Stogumber, though recognizable as a type, very nearly loses his essential humanity and becomes a cardboard outline. Just as we are giving him up, his utter breakdown when he sees what he has done restores him to us as a human being whose lack of imagination about cruelty we all share in some degree. The miracle in the first act where acceptance of Joan's mission sets all the hens a-laying is pure farce. Yet a serious miracle would only have detracted from the changing of the wind in Act Two. Moreover, if Heaven interfered too obviously, Joan's personality, which develops through the play, would have less to do. The farcical miracle sets the audience in a roar without diminishing Joan.

Another interesting side of *Saint Joan* is the increasing range of Shaw's characters. Never until recently had he

Sybil Thorndike as Saint Joan. London, 1924.

tried to portray old people. Captain Shotover, his most successful portrait till now, is so weird an example that he hardly counts. The Inquisitor, however, demonstrates to perfection the cautious reasoning of an elderly mind, the anxiety to smooth away objections before they are uttered, the scrupulous kindliness which has nothing whatever to do with personal feeling. It is the Inquisitor and this fortunate restraint which remind us that *Saint Joan* is the work of a man in his middle and late sixties. So far no sign appears that Shaw is worn out.

Had he merely been writing a play about Joan of Arc, the tragedy of her death would have made a suitable ending. Since Shaw is always talking about his own time, he is using history to point out important truths which are always valid. *Saint Joan* is a conflict between an inspired individual and human institutions. Shaw is careful to take both sides. He is not an anarchist; and he believes that government must control the individual, even while he recognizes that Joan is right. It is this theme which dictates the epilogue, raising Joan's death above a personal tragedy. Church and politicians rehabilitate Joan, and centuries after her death she is made a saint. The institutions which had condemned her prove their good intentions by admitting their fault. All worship Joan, but the conflict which brought about her death has not been solved. When she suggests returning to earth, it is obvious that she will suffer the same fate, none standing by her. Thus the true tragedy is contained in Joan's last exclamation: "O God that madest this beautiful earth, when will it be ready to receive Thy saints? How long, O Lord, how long?" Shaw had a message for his generation, and it was unthinkable that he should write a major work for any other reason.

He had at last written a play which pleased everybody. Catholics and Protestants alike felt he had done them justice. Freethinkers recognized his lofty theme. Critics praised *Saint Joan*, and the general public flocked to see it in greater numbers than had been drawn even by *Pygmalion*. Rapidly translated into French and German, *Saint Joan* drew royalties from the continent of Europe even exceeding those Shaw had lost there through nine years of war and inflation. In one language or another, it went around the world, bringing Shaw a reputation beside which his previous one looked petty. People wrote to him from all over the globe, asking for favors, small and large, or wanting advice on every intimate matter, from choosing a religion to taking a wife. He had arrived at the same moment at the positions of successful writer and elder statesman, so that the reverence which he now commanded was greater than it would have been if one had come before the other.

He took what measures he could to defend himself. His secretary had a number of printed postcards in different colors which were sent in answer to various classes of letters. A pink — or later a blue — card informed autograph collectors that Shaw would not respond to "unsportsmanlike requests by strangers to forge his own signature for their benefit as legitimate collecting." He had signed, he pointed out, in the course of an active life "ample material for the proper exercise of their peculiar industry." Even this severe rebuke, however, was not always adequate. One ingenious gentleman wrote to say that he had invented a pill and wanted permission to call it "The G.B.S." This drew a curt and indignant answer in the sage's own hand, threatening suit. Gleefully the recipient sent his thanks. There never had been a pill, and he had obtained what he wanted.

Another postcard went out refusing to autograph copies of his books. If he replied to such requests, he would be overwhelmed by speculators who purchased his books at the standard price, got them signed, and sold at a profit. He therefore reserved his signature for his personal gifts.

Writers in search of a preface by Shaw to their own works were told that they were requesting some months of hard professional work for nothing. Moreover, his prefaces owed their value to the general expectation that the works he thus favored would be good. If his endorsement became indiscriminate, it would become meaningless.

Another card in pink requested that Mr. Bernard Shaw be excused from the appeals he received daily "from charitable institutions, religious sects and churches, inventors, Utopian writers . . . parents unable to afford secondary education for their children: in short everybody and every enterprise in financial straits of any sort." All these, the card pointed out, were founded on the idea that Mr. Shaw was a millionaire. Actually, all his income except enough to meet his permanent responsibilities was confiscated by the Exchequer and redistributed to those with smaller tax-free incomes or applied to general purposes by which everyone benefited. This response exaggerated his taxes. Shaw was becoming a rich man despite them, though no millionaire. One sign of increasing age, however, was a fear of going bankrupt which no study of his bank balance could allay. Its cause lay deep in his uncertain past; and it is only remarkable that an upbringing such as his did not produce many more phobias. In any case, he cared little for organized charity, preferring to give his money to institutions like the Royal Academy of Dramatic Art, where it would have a positive effect.

Mail still came pouring in, addressed to: "George Bernard Shaw, Esq., Philosopher and Writer, London"; to "George Bernard Shaw, the one and only"; addressed even to: His Excellence, Dr., the Hon., or Sir Bernard Shaw "Wherever he lives." An orange postcard replied that though Mr. Shaw was always glad to receive interesting letters, he seldom had time to answer because his correspondence was so large. This indeed was literally true. Those people to whom he did write in his own hand waited longer and longer, while postcards went out to the less favored with prompt dispatch.

He was always insistent on getting his royalties, not because he needed them, but because other authors did. He would not allow his example to be used to put pressure on writers who wanted the money. Thus a postcard, white this time, informed amateur groups that private or school performances of his plays were privileged, but that "if numerous spectators are invited to witness them in large buildings they may damage the Author." It added that "admission without legal payment is not a valid defense in such legal action as may ensue." His press-clipping service sent him reviews from local papers, and he did in fact protest if any performance was given without the proper royalty payment.

Invitations to speak, to open bazaars, to take the chair at a meeting, or to make an appeal for charity were answered that Mr. Shaw was now obliged to restrict his platform activities to special occasions. Public dinners had never been favorites of his, and he declined one in honor of Ramsay MacDonald in the following terms: "Considering that the man has been Prime Minister of England,

I should have thought his eminence had been noticed. If the dinner is a success, I suggest that it be followed by another to acknowledge the piety of the Pope, yet another to emphasize the mathematical talent of Einstein, and a final one to call attention to the existence of milestones on the Dover Road."

Ramsay MacDonald, whom he had known well as a former Fabian, became Prime Minister for the second time in 1929, at which time Sidney Webb accepted a peerage — not because he valued the honor or believed in peers, but because the Labour Party had hardly any representation in the House of Lords. Shaw was offered a peerage for the same reason, but he declined it. He was instrumental in having various other people given knighthoods, but refused to add "Sir" to his own name. He even turned down the Order of Merit, which has only twenty-four living members, involves no change of name, and is awarded solely on a basis of distinction. The initials had come to mean Old Man, he said, and he did not feel old, though now in his seventies. Truth was that he already was so distinguished that official honors could do nothing for him.

One honor he could not avoid without being ungracious. He was awarded the Nobel Prize for Literature in 1925, though he desperately tried to avoid it. In particular, he did not believe in money prizes for authors already too well known to need the cash. The matter was finally arranged by his handing over the money to finance the translation of Swedish literary works into English. His action, however, gave enormous encouragement to begging letter writers, particularly from the United States, land of enterprise, where people hastened to lay their financial problems before the man who was rich enough to do without the Nobel Prize. Shaw was forced, he said, to practice "a complicated facial expression which combines universal benevolence with a savage determination not to save any American from ruin by a remittance of five hundred dollars."

Nineteen twenty-six was the year of his seventieth birthday. He was just recovering from his only serious illness since his marriage and felt in no mood to receive the avalanche of congratulations which now fell on him. In his mother's household, birthdays had been ignored; and he had never accustomed himself to the fact that people would remember whether he liked it or not. Telegrams, birthday cakes, presents of all kinds, more appeals for money poured in at such a rate that he felt, he said, as though he were being stoned. The postcard that went out in response said: "Mr. Bernard Shaw implores his friends and readers not to celebrate his birthdays nor even to mention them to him. It is easy to write one letter or send one birthday cake, but the arrival of hundreds of them together is a calamity that is not the less dreaded because it occurs only once a year."

Worse than anything were the number of letters that he had to answer in person from eminent people all over the civilized globe. Deliberately Shaw had set out to be a prophet to his generation, but he had never imagined the practical problems of success. His burden was heavy enough to excuse any man for feeling old.

1926–1933

The Apple Cart

L UCY C ARR S HAW had died in 1920 as a result of a breakdown brought about by insomnia and the strain of the
zeppelin air raids of World War I. After long separation
from her husband, she had divorced him, but finding he
was lonely, she let him spend his evenings at her fireside
until he died. Lucy had made little of her talent, yet she
had a number of friends. With her brother she was on
good terms, but never intimate. During her illness, he
called on her from time to time, and on the last occasion
found her in bed. When she told him that she was
dying, he took her hand and held it. Presently, while he
still did so, she died. Though Lucy was too like her
mother ever to have cared deeply for anyone, she had
fascinated many.

The Shaws had now no close relation left but Charlotte's sister, who lived on her husband's Irish estate. In
1898, Lady Cholmondeley had refused to meet her new
brother-in-law, indignant that Charlotte should disgrace
herself by marrying a penniless bohemian. The situation
was an impossible one between sisters, so that presently a

meeting was arranged. Lady Cholmondeley fell victim to Shaw's charm before she realized who he was; and ever afterwards, their relationship was friendly. In the mid-twenties she wrote to ask a favor. Would he be so good as to write her a short explanation of the basic principles of socialism? She wanted it for her rural women's club, of which she was president.

Delighted to oblige, Shaw set to work right away. The more he wrote, however, the more he found to say, so that presently he became immersed in a full-length book instead of a pamphlet. By the time that he finished, he was almost sorry he had started what proved to be a complex task. He had been studying, speaking, writing propaganda for socialism during many years. It was his answer to the problem of improving human institutions. It even gave hope of bettering human nature, though he was too intelligent to think that when the people got their rights they would automatically be perfect. In all the time that Shaw had crusaded for socialism, he had never tried to explain to perfectly ignorant persons what he meant. Given his facility with words, it was no wonder that he could not pack his life's experience into the brief compass that his sister-in-law had requested. *The Intelligent Woman's Guide to Socialism* is a solid book.

Beautifully though it is written, *The Intelligent Woman* does not take its place among the great classics of socialist literature. People do not go to it for the reasons that they go to *Das Kapital*. There is nothing original in it. Nor is it free from the verbosity which can make Shaw difficult reading. "Oh, for goodness' sake don't tell me everything or we shall never have done," he imagines the Intelligent Woman exclaiming at one point. It is impossible to feel that he always regards this simple warning. The Intelligent Woman has to learn what capitalism is, into what classes it divides society, why all of them degenerate in one way or another, what taxes do to redress the balance, and why they fail. She goes through a short history of banking, the money market, trade-unionism, the industrial revolution, the national debt, the party system, and various substitutes for socialism, such as state capitalism and cooperative ventures. Convinced at last that socialism is the only remedy, she has to examine the question of how to bring it about — by revolution or by parliamentary methods.

What then is socialism? It is a system in which the state is the only owner of capital and the only employer. It is to Shaw a system in which everybody has exactly the same income. Some radicals consider that income should be distributed according to the amount of work performed. This, he thinks, is not practicable because work varies in kind and quality. Many people, moreover, have a compulsion to work; yet there is no reason to reward them for this or to penalize others because their metabolism is different. Some say that income should be proportionate to need. This subsidizes the parasite on society who will not work. Shaw is ready to punish Weary Willie if he will not do his daily stint, though Willie is welcome to spend his leisure lying on his back.

What Shaw is not willing to compromise with is the competitive instinct. Everybody likes to do better than his neighbor. This will have to go, and the only possible substitute is that each will prefer his own job to his neighbor's. Actually, the difficulties of fitting a man to the right job are immense. Shaw has no answer to the problem beyond the testing processes which we can work out, save a certain optimism from which no reformer is free. He is confident that so many bad motives will be superseded that superior ones will have a chance.

The charm of *The Intelligent Woman* consists in the wisdom and eloquence which lie embedded in its rhetoric.

> Whenever your sympathies are strongly stirred on behalf of some cruelly ill-used . . . persons . . . your generous indignation attributes all sorts of virtues to them and . . . vices to those who oppress them. But the blunt truth is that ill-used people are worse than well-used people: indeed this is at bottom the only good reason why we should not allow anyone to be ill-used. If I thought you would be made a better woman by ill treatment I should do my best to have you ill treated.

Or: The virtues that feed on suffering are very questionable virtues. There are people who positively wallow in hospitals and charitable societies and Relief Funds and the like . . . There will always be plenty of need in the world for kindness; but it should not be wasted on preventable starvation and disease.

Or: Equalization of income will be brought about, not by every woman making it her private busi-

ness, but by every woman making it her public
business: that is by law. And it will not be a
single law, but a long series of laws.

It is not until even the Intelligent Woman is exhausted
that she is allowed in the last seventy pages of the book
to examine what socialism will do for individual liberty,
for marriage, for the family, and for religion. Even then
she has to clear up yet another set of possible confusions
before she comes at last to the peroration, which has great
dignity.

> The coveted distinction of lady and gentle-
> man, instead of . . . meaning persons who never
> condescend to do anything for themselves that
> they can possibly put on others . . . will at last
> take on a simple and noble meaning . . . For
> them the base woman will be she who takes from
> her country more than she gives to it; the com-
> mon person will be she who does no more than
> replace what she takes; and the lady will be she
> who, generously overearning her income, leaves
> the nation in her debt and the world a better
> place than she found it.

This is a splendid ideal, and its expression is only
spoiled by the fact that one cannot read it clearly without
making omissions. It has one other drawback: Shaw already said it in a speech in 1913. This last may not be a
criticism, but it is surely a sign he was getting old.

In 1929, Barry Jackson started a six-weeks' drama festival for Shaw in Malvern, opening with *Back to Methuselah, Heartbreak House, Caesar and Cleopatra,* and *The*

Apple Cart, a play which Shaw had recently written in six weeks of concentrated work. It was his first original play since *Saint Joan*, and he was now seventy-three. From the point of view of the creative artist, it is unfortunate that he should have spent the last six years on *The Intelligent Woman* and a splendidly generous gesture for a friend. Trebitsch, the Austrian playwright who had translated his own works had been ruined by the postwar inflation. Shaw, though no great German scholar, translated and adapted his *Jitta's Atonement* in order to earn him needed pounds and dollars. Earlier, Shaw could better have afforded the time, since it stood to reason that his creative powers would not remain forever at their peak. *The Apple Cart*, as it happens, is a good rather than a great play. It displays much of the old skill and is in addition an interesting reflection of Shaw's thought on politics. Indeed, *The Apple Cart* in many ways sets the tone for a series of later, but far inferior, works of the aging playwright.

Barry Jackson had brought the old man back to the theater again; and for most of the next ten years he was able to produce a new Shaw play as the climax of each season. Most of these thereafter went on to London, where *The Apple Cart* at least was highly successful. In the meantime Shaw, who was intensely loyal to his personal friends, did his best for Jackson and Malvern. Not only did he rehearse his plays, but he actually stayed at the Malvern Hotel throughout the season, well aware that he was the greatest draw of the whole affair. It meant being never left alone, being mobbed by admirers, being followed even on tramps over the Malvern Hills. Not until he was eighty-one did he compromise by staying at a distance and driving over to see the plays that he wanted.

All the London critics came up in a body to Malvern to preview *The Apple Cart* at its dress rehearsal. Public expectation was on tiptoe, and it was not entirely disappointed. *The Apple Cart* was certainly not another *Saint Joan*, but it had plenty of interest, particularly so in England.

The hero of *The Apple Cart* is King Magnus, who, as he himself admits, is Shaw disguised rather thinly as the constitutional monarch of a country whose political life exactly corresponds to England's. Here, with the Labour Party in control and opinion veering ever further to the Left, the King is naturally in an awkward position. Some advantages he still has: he is permanent, while ministers come and go; and his opinion is still influential. He has been speaking out on various issues, and his Cabinet is quite determined to muzzle him. It is obvious that if they insist, they have the power to reduce the King to a nonentity, a rubber stamp. He tries to divide them, to charm them, to persuade them, all in vain. Eventually he threatens to resign, become a commoner, found a party, fight an election, and turn them all out of office. They are really afraid that he could, and they give way utterly.

This rather simple plot becomes a vehicle for a great deal Shaw desires to say about the government of England. He has no use for the democratic system in which the ignorant masses choose between people who court their favor by making promises which they either cannot

or do not intend to carry out. He has put up with it all his life. He has even told the Intelligent Woman that Parliament, which is elected precisely in this way, will have to carry through the socialist revolution by legal means. All the same, Shaw likes neither the system nor the kind of politician it turns up. Proteus, the Prime Minister of *The Apple Cart*, whose people come from Scotland, was the Labour Prime Minister Ramsay MacDonald, of whom Shaw said to Hesketh Pearson: "He was not the sort of man one could like." Proteus is vain and a poseur, but instinctively he understands intrigue. His Cabinet colleagues are some able and some not, but political jobbery has tied all their hands. In particular, even the well-meaning ones are helpless in the hands of Breakages Limited, which symbolizes Capitalism. Breakages has a vested interest in producing things that will wear out, are accident-prone, or simply inefficient. The politicians all hold their jobs on sufferance. Breakages controls them by the power of big business and money, so that real improvements cannot be made, while useful inventions are bought up by the combine and disappear.

The only one of the whole lot who is really fit to govern is Magnus. In effect, Shaw is saying that the hereditary principle may on occasion turn up a sound man, whereas a democratic election under modern conditions never does. This devastating pronouncement is all the more impressive because it comes at the end of a long life, much of which has been spent working with political parties to put through reforms. Now this was a notion that Shaw had always to some extent held, even though he was able

Still spry at seventy-four.
A birthday photograph in 1930.

at the same time to respect the competence of a democratic working body like the Borough Council of St. Pancras. Hitherto, however, he had remained comparatively
silent on the subject. What had inspired *The Apple Cart*
was Shaw's disillusion with political developments since
the war, which were driving him, despite his Fabian beliefs, to the despair of Parliament and even of the Parliamentary Labour Party.

Nothing had gone well in Great Britain since the war.
Demobilization had thrown too many men on the labor
market without the state's providing public funds for
their further education, which might have gone far to
solve the problem. England's trade and financial position
had been worsened by the war. Her industrial equipment
was overworked and out-of-date. Her coal mines were
in a state of terrible depression and needed a complete
overhaul. There were small communities in which everyone was on relief because a factory, or a shipyard, or a
mine had closed forever. Only the most drastic measures
would have helped because overall planning ran at every
turn into vested interests of people who either wanted to
keep things as they were or grab government money.

Two Labour governments had taken office during this
time, the first in 1924, and the second in 1929. In neither
case did Labour have a true majority, so that it was able
to put through measures only with the aid of the Liberals.
Thus socialism had never had a chance, while Labour
politicians, made tame and cautious by experience, had
reacted in unexpected ways. Ramsay MacDonald, for
instance, liked to play the great man. He was making

friends with people whom he never would have met years ago, and who did not share his socialist convictions. Beatrice and Sidney had been concerned in 1924 because Labour ministers and their wives were at a disadvantage through not having sufficient social experience. By now the worry was all the other way; they had too much. It was not unnatural for a Fabian like Shaw, after watching and waiting for Parliamentary influence through a long lifetime, to feel something like despair at last. The Labour Party had come of age, and still nothing got done.

For reasons such as these, *The Apple Cart,* coming at the very start of the Great Depression and preceding the international turmoil of the thirties, has a real significance in Shaw's development. None of the ideas expressed are new to him. It is notable, for instance, that in *Back to Methuselah* the stupidity and wickedness of the Short-livers are political. What really matters about *The Apple Cart* is that just at the moment when terrible troubles on an international scale are about to boil up, Shaw's lack of faith in the democratic process has come to the point where he cannot contain it. He has no conviction which can carry him forward through the troubles that are coming, unless he can imagine some way to improve on democracy. This is *Heartbreak House* all over again, with the difference that *Heartbreak House* is chiefly about something past, whereas *The Apple Cart* shows the present as it is, suggesting no hope for the future.

The Apple Cart, however, is not entirely about politics. There is an interlude in the middle which King Magnus spends with his mistress, the incident having no con-

nection with the rest of the play beyond the fact that
kings are often thought of as people who *do* have mis-
tresses. Notwithstanding, the scene between Magnus
and his Orinthia has charm and plays well on the stage.
The professional circles in which dramatists and actors
move are not very large, so that it is not surprising to hear
that Edith Evans, who was cast for Orinthia, soon informed Mrs. Patrick Campbell that she was playing *her*.

After the run of *Pygmalion* was over, Shaw and Mrs.
Pat had parted company. She was now a married woman
whose husband was soon serving in the armed forces of
World War I. Shaw, as we have seen, was not publishing
plays at that time. For part of the war, Stella had been
away on an American tour. Occasional letters had passed
between the pair about this arrangement or that. Their
tone had been the familiar one of old acquaintances
rather than old lovers. Age, however, was beginning to
deal hardly with Stella. Even Ellen Terry had found it
difficult to make the transition from leading lady to elderly roles. Stella's temperament, her extravagance, and
her poor judgment when it came to managing her own
company created endless difficulties for her. After *Pygmalion* she did not score a single success until just before
The Apple Cart in 1929, when she was triumphant in *The
Matriarch*, a powerful drama about an older woman.

Amid all her vagaries, Stella had been a proud and
devoted mother to her two children. Her son was killed in
the war in 1918. Her marriage to Cornwallis West lasted
a year longer and might have broken up before, had he
not been absent from her during most of the time.

Lonely, aging, and in financial straits, she was growing desperate. In 1919 she had angled in vain for the part of Hesione in *Heartbreak House*. Hesione is a dark charmer, founded, as Shaw later admitted, on memories of Stella. Lilith, the Serpent, in *Back to Methuselah* was another such part. Again she did not get it.

In 1921, she thought of raising money by publishing her memoirs. As it was common knowledge that she possessed intimate letters from a number of well-known people, the project extracted a substantial advance from publishers. Stella wrote to Shaw, Barrie and various others, asking permission to publish some of their correspondence with her.

Shaw was in a quandary. Considering Charlotte's jealousy of Stella, he hardly desired to see his letters made public. On the other hand, he was a man incapable of malice. He had suffered when Stella threw him off eight years ago, but that hurt was long healed. In the *Pygmalion* rehearsals she had tried his patience to the utmost; but she had been glorious in the part. He remembered Stella as a marvelous creature; he admired her still; and he was aware that she certainly needed the money. If some innocuous letters were published in combination with similar tributes from all sorts of other people, Charlotte might perceive there was nothing special in them. Trusting to Stella's discretion, he gave his permission.

Almost immediately he found himself in hot water. None of Stella's other correspondents except Barrie had been equally complaisant. Thus far from finding himself one among dozens, Shaw stood out almost alone.

Stella, moreover, was bound to give her publishers and public some value for their money. The consequence was that when she sent him copies of the letters she proposed to insert, he was appalled.

In vain he wrote her, heatedly denouncing the publicity as vulgar, exclaiming that Charlotte would be hurt, even threatening that Cornwallis West might sue for divorce. He would allow amusing scraps, drawing-room gallantries, and serious passages fit for publication. He accused her of deliberate malice against "the author who . . . treated you on the stage with brutality and savagery which you can never forget." He reminded her that he felt a good deal more than she, and that he still did. She was doing a terrible thing.

Stella eluded his reproaches. "What abominable letters you do write me Joey dear! — But you did *once* write me a letter that I am going to leave to the Nation!" She pointed out that as a love affair the whole thing had been pretence. "Never did I think your love making other than what it was — sympathy, kindness, and the wit and folly of genius." Presently she lost her patience and showed her claws. She would publish *exactly* what she liked and had his letter giving permission. *"So you be civil."*

He let her go ahead, it is hard to say from what motive. Perhaps he felt compassion because she was desperate. Possibly he thought the publicity of trying to stop her would be worse than what he must endure if he did not. She had shown some restraint, after all, if not enough. Unfortunately Charlotte seems to have taken the view that she had not shown any.

Even after this, he could not find it in him to feel resentment. A year or so later he wrote, "I forgive you the letters because there is a star somewhere on which you were right about them; and on that star we two should have been born." When *Saint Joan* opened in 1924, she telegraphed him in congratulation, and he answered; but he had not yet said his last word on the letters. "If you knew the trouble those unlucky letters made for me, you would understand a lot of things. I don't regret it; and it doesn't matter as it got you out of your difficulties for a moment; but O Lord, Stella, it mustn't happen again until we are both dead." She had many other letters.

By 1928, she was in low water again, and he advised her to sell his letters, warning that though she had a right to do this, they could not be published without his permission. But Stella merely replied she was not starving and could not bargain with his lovely letters. "Splendid!" he told her. "All those flags flying; but that is how the Stella Stellarum would go down. I am not easy." She consented to sell the set of his books that he had autographed for her.

Matters were in this state between Stella and Joey the Clown who turned all things to mockery when Edith Evans informed Mrs. Pat that she was Orinthia.

It was Stella's turn to be agitated now. She pestered Shaw for a copy of the play, uncertain whether to demand the role or to be angry at being exposed on the stage. He put her off. He did not have a spare copy. As for the part, she could not have it. "You would most certainly play the devil with the whole production and perhaps make me

behave badly and leave me ten years older." He could
not go through the experience of *Pygmalion* again. About
his conduct in the matter, he was simply defiant. Was he
not Joey? Had he not said in the beginning that he would
write about this thing? And did he not always write about
everything that he experienced?

He offered to read her the play, perceiving probably that
it was better to talk it over than to squabble by letter.
When he did so, her indignation changed to boiling
fury. Magnus's Orinthia has a fancy to be queen. She is
fascinating and thinks she would grace a crown, while the
queen is very dull. Magnus will have nothing to do with
this proposition. He points out to Orinthia that he does
not look on her in the same light as he looks on the queen.
An insult to his wife is like a blow in his own face. Some-
how or other, he cannot get excited about Orinthia's dignity. He even remarks that she has had two husbands
already who have not been able to get on with her. Her
relationship with him is one of innocent flirtation and has
nothing to do with the queen.

We may acquit Shaw of any desire for revenge in this
episode. The superior attitude of Magnus throughout is
dictated by the exigencies of the play . . . and possibly
by consideration for Charlotte. Nothing, however, could
have been more mortifying to Stella's pride or a more
complete rebuttal of what she had published in her memoirs. Joey even had referred in that insulting way to her
two husbands. She made him alter the passage but, protesting that it did not really apply, he changed it little.
She was, however, chiefly offended by the scene's climax.

Shaw had always during the course of his visits to Stella insisted on being home when he was expected. He had never missed a train yet, he wrote on one occasion. She must not let him hurt one "to whom I am bound by all the bonds except the bond of the child to the dark lady." Stella, always jealous when he deferred to Charlotte, had deliberately tried to make him late. When she found that persuasion failed and his attention was never distracted from the time, she actually caught him by the wrists and forced him to tug himself free. Finally she threw her arms about him and brought him to the floor, where they thrashed about in an undignified fashion until he tore himself away. This episode now appeared in *The Apple Cart* when Orinthia tried to make King Magnus late for tea with his wife. In similar fashion had Jenny Patterson walked onstage in *The Philanderer* in 1894 to attack Florence Farr. It was quite literally true that anything dramatic which happened to Joey the Clown would appear on the stage. He was apologetic about his own nature. "You are the vampire and I the victim; yet it is I who suck your blood and fatten on it whilst you lose everything."

Stella raged, while Shaw protested that only a few people knew about these private matters between himself and her. The rumors which he admitted were going around were due to Stella's own indiscretion. In the event, she had to put up with the play in silence. Charlotte, who may possibly have felt vindicated, said nothing either. She knew "The Genius," as she used to call her husband, would grind whatever came to his mill.

Even now Shaw was not done with Stella. In 1931, he gave permission for his letters to Ellen Terry to be published for the benefit of her heirs. They were immediately recognized as a classic in correspondence, and they made a great deal of money. Stella's last success was behind her now. She was in her middle sixties, and the future was beginning to look grim. She had a hundred and twenty-five letters from Shaw. Why should she not publish them, too?

No, he said. He explained patiently that she could sell the letters, for which she said she had been offered five hundred dollars apiece. No one, however, could publish them during his lifetime without his permission. Stella, who had gone to Hollywood by now and was not getting parts, replied with fresh propositions, opinions from American lawyers, fabulous offers from publishers. This time she had met her match, and no meant no.

By 1937, she had given up. She was living on a small allowance made by a friend in a cheap hotel in New York. She could not return to England because it involved a six-months' quarantine for her dog, and she could not bear to expose him to it. "Believe me, a new hat is an event," she wrote to Joey. He for his part sent her own letters back in order that the collection might have an increased value if she sold it. Still, however, she would not part with it, especially the letter which ought to be written in letters of gold. She thought it was time he forgave her for her conduct in the *Pygmalion* rehearsals. He never imagined her difficulties then. After all, she was twenty-five years too old for Eliza. That would make her forty-three, replied Joey, tongue in cheek. "I was the more deceived." Almost certainly he knew quite well she had been forty-eight.

Stella died in 1940 in France. She was seventy-five and had lost the will to live. She left the letters which she had treasured so long to her daughter and grandchildren, her sole estate. For their benefit they were published later on, when Charlotte was dead.

1930–1938

A Bloodless Old Age

Bᴇʀɴᴀʀᴅ Sʜᴀᴡ had never formed intimacies with ease, since he preferred to meet people on his own terms during a brief call or weekend visit. Now that he had become so famous, many hostesses were eager to entertain him, promising company which they hoped he would enjoy. Persistent among these was Nancy, Viscountess Astor, a member of Parliament and much in the news. Lady Astor was a little woman, American-born, of boundless energy and considerable charm. She entertained largely at Cliveden, her husband's country estate on the Thames not far from Windsor. No social circle would have seemed less to Shaw's taste, and he repulsed every effort of Lady Astor until chance threw them together, when he found that he liked her.

Perhaps her vitality intrigued him. Possibly she enjoyed playing the old game of harmless flirtation which he was not too ancient to pursue in laughing fashion. Certainly she was skillful enough in getting to Cliveden people whom he wanted to meet. It may have been pleasanter to make contacts there than in the London flat or over a

weekend at Ayot. At all events, he liked to go to Cliveden;
and they met often. They had certain prejudices in common, though she was more ardent than he. He did not
drink liquor; she was a fiery teetotaler. He was skeptical
about medical knowledge; she was a Christian Scientist.
These superficial likenesses of opinion, however, could not
conceal the fact that they made an odd pair. Nancy Astor
belonged to the extreme right wing of wealthy con-
servatism, a section which, without being fascist, supported fascist notions. One of the social lions of whom
Cliveden made much in the middle thirties was Ribben-
trop, Hitler's ambassador. Such a hostess, no matter how
personally charming, might well seem a strange friend for
an old Fabian.

The circumstances of the times were throwing the two
together. In his disgust at the postwar state of Europe,
his despair of Parliamentary democracy, Shaw was ready
to put up with extreme remedies. When Mussolini
took over the government of Italy and threw his opponents
into concentration camps, Shaw hailed him as a great man
for bringing order out of chaos. It was true that Italian
trains now ran on time and that unemployment was being
reduced by public works. When Italian liberals protested
the arrest of their friends, the beatings, and the castor oil,
Shaw airily answered that the British were far more brutal.
Did they not have prisons? Was not flogging still a punishment for certain sorts of offenses? Concentration camps
were a British invention during the Boer War, when whole
villages had been interned in order to put down guerrillas.
As usual, Shaw had chosen to annoy rather than to con-

vince; but he had a real quarrel with Italian and British liberals alike. Disgusted with both, he was disposed to favor anyone who had a different approach to government.

This attitude of Shaw's was not a new one; it reflected his interest in exceptional men like Napoleon and Caesar. Mussolini's origins were fairly humble, as Napoleon's had been. He too was against those in power and anxious to distribute some of their wealth through the body politic. As a Fabian, Shaw welcomed Mussolini in the hope that better organization would lead Italy one step nearer to the ultimate end of socialism. In this, however, he parted company with the bulk of the Fabians and Labour Party. Nor would he or could he perceive that the twentieth-century dictators were far more sinister figures than the well-meaning nineteenth-century liberals he was used to.

With a common interest in fascism, though for different reasons, Shaw and Nancy Astor grew closer together. Eventually they even undertook a trip on which, it might be imagined, they would disagree every moment of the way. In 1931, unaccompanied by Charlotte, Shaw set out with Lord and Lady Astor and the Marquess of Lothian, a liberal politician, on a visit to Russia.

The Russian Revolution had not excited the Fabians greatly. They were not Marxian socialists and they did not believe in Lenin's methods, except insofar as he made some compromises in favor of gradualism. Of Stalin, like the rest of the world, they knew very little. By 1931, however, when Western civilization was in the grip of the Great Depression, Russia was climbing out of hers, which had — owing to Stalin's ill-advised haste in setting up collective farms — ruined agriculture and starved to death some million peasant proprietors. In 1931, Stalin's Five-Year Plan was beginning to show results, while the great purge of the thirties, which destroyed perhaps fifteen million more people, was not under way. It seemed for the moment as though the upheavals of the revolution were at last over. It was a good time to go to Russia and find out what socialism had achieved there.

Shaw liked everything he saw. No judge of food, he con-

Shaw with
Lady Astor.

sidered cabbage soup and black bread an excellent diet.
No judge of clothes, he did not care if everybody was
cheaply and badly dressed, as long as no one looked better than his fellows. Shops were empty, but as he never
saw anything in London which tempted him to buy, this
did not matter. Unaccustomed to the physiognomy of Rus-
sians, he jumped to the conclusion that their expressions
reflected a lack of pressure, due to the absence of capitalism. He was fascinated by Tsarist palaces turned into re-
sort hotels for favored workers, by public museums, col-

*Shaw and Lady Astor sitting with Russian authors
on their tour in 1931.*

lective farms, and state-owned factories. The Soviet government really had some things to show; and it was very well aware of its visitors' importance. The party was even given an interview by Stalin, who had not consented to see the British ambassador.

In the highest spirits, Shaw delivered a speech which was widely reported to the effect that in Russia he felt at home. At last in his own time he had seen socialism erecting an entirely new edifice out of the state. He saw the better side of it — the modern methods of farming which the new collectives would make possible, the tremendous efforts to transform an illiterate population into a reading population in a single generation. In England, he had been more concerned to criticize schools and prisons than to keep abreast of pioneer work being done. Thus he compared Russia not with England as she was, but as she had been.

He talked to Stalin for nearly three hours and found him charming. He did not think it curious that the official interpreter was too scared of the great man to do his work. Recognizing Stalin's power, Shaw could not help investing him with his own restless desire for world improvement. Used to thinking that he was right, he retained the impression that he could sum up a modern dictator in one meeting.

Full of enthusiasm when he came home, he told Beatrice and Sidney that the promised land of which they had been dreaming for nearly fifty years was Russia after all. His words came at a moment of intense disillusion for the

Webbs. The Labour government had not been able to stave off financial collapse. Britain went off the gold standard; and Ramsay MacDonald, the Labour leader, deserted his party to form a coalition with the Conservatives in which he remained in office as Prime Minister and puppet of a conservative administration. This act of treachery — for such it was — split the Labour Party and left Sidney marooned in the House of Lords, which he had only entered in the hope of being some use to a socialist government. In the circumstances, the Webbs were eager to go and see for themselves.

They descended on Russia in their usual well-planned way with lists of questions, places to see, government publications which they could carry home for further study. In Russia, the Webbs were almost as well known as Bernard Shaw, though all three were considered a weak and washy pink, not genuine red. It suited Stalin at this time to gain good opinions, so that the Webbs were provided with interpreters, guides, and documents by the trunkload. No sort of restraints were laid on them, and they were not prevented from interviewing where they pleased — through their interpreters.

The Webbs came back far more enthusiastic than even Shaw had been and were accompanied by a ton of documents. Applying their usual methods to these with the aid of translators, they produced a heavy book in praise of Soviet Russia. They had not reckoned with the fact that Russian statistics were not reliable just because they were in print, or that Soviet reports were affected by everyone's

desire to please his superior. Nor had they, supremely
ignorant of what did not concern them, any inkling of how
much that the Soviets claimed had been done by the Tsar-
ists.

In any event, toward the end of their long and useful
lives, the Webbs were granted a gleam of hope that their
ideals were going into action. They did not join any communist party or pledge themselves to revolution in England. They merely thought that sooner or later the progress in Russia would sweep even England into socialism.
Meanwhile, whatever was Russian must be good; and
they felt it their duty to preach this gospel.

This directly affected Shaw, who was in a more vulnera-
ble position than the Webbs because their importance
was not the kind that makes news. As the great purge in
Russia gathered momentum, as countless men were put
to death, as fifteen million or more were sent as slaves to
labor in subhuman conditions in camps near the Arctic
Circle, it mattered little to the general public that the
Webbs were ardently pro-Russian. Shaw, on the other
hand, was forced to deny or to justify all that he had
said.

He chose to justify. He had always been a tender-
hearted humanitarian with a hardheaded streak. He
would not eat animals because he thought it cannibalism,
yet he admitted that tigers and microbes of measles and
other such creatures must be destroyed. Similarly, he had
always denounced prison as organized torture unworthy
of a civilized nation; but he recognized that if remedial

methods proved hopeless, something had to be done about a criminal. His solution was to put incorrigible people kindly but firmly to death. He now extended this argument to prove that "liquidation" by the Communist regime of its enemies was no punishment, but justice. He seemed to imagine that because he used the modern term, the deed was painless, or that a "labor camp" was no prison at all. He even ignored the fact that hosts of innocent people were swept away on bare shadow of suspicion.

It is disillusioning to see Shaw writing in the preface to one of his plays in 1935 about a Russian Commissar called Djerjinsky, "He was not a homicidally disposed person; but when it fell to his lot to make the Russian trains run at all costs, he had to force himself to shoot a station master who found it easier to drop telegrams into the wastepaper basket than to attend to them. And it was this gentle Djerjinsky who, unable to endure the duties of an executioner . . . organized the Tcheka." Now the Tcheka was the Russian political police, as bloodstained an organization as the infamous SS became under Hitler. Shaw might as well have praised the squeamishness of Himmler.

This kindly, inhuman tone may serve to remind us of the Inquisitor in *Saint Joan*, so compassionate, so impersonal, and so old. Shaw is seventy-nine in 1935, and it seems to cost him never a qualm to defend the agony inflicted upon millions. The play which he produced at this time, called *The Simpleton of the Unexpected Isles*, is partly an inferior *Heartbreak House* and partly a vision

of the Day of Judgment in which everyone who is no use
is liquidated and disappears.

> Stock Exchange closes: only two members left.
> House of Commons decimated: only fourteen
> members to be found, none of Cabinet rank . . .
> Mayfair a desert: six hotels left without a single
> guest . . . Crowded intercession service at
> Westminster Abbey brought to a close by disap-
> pearance of the congregation at such a rate that
> the rest fled, leaving the dean preaching to the
> choir.

All this is fooling, yet, alas, it is no longer very pointed
or funny.

He wrote his preface to *The Simpleton* in the Far East.
Age had by no means sated Charlotte's appetite for
travel. It had merely taught her that a cruise ship is less
wearing than a train, while the publicity attendant on
her husband's comings and goings was less on shipboard
than in a series of hotels. As for Shaw, he had learned to
protect himself with the minimum of trouble. Selecting an
unattached middle-aged lady who was dying to meet
such a great celebrity, he planted his deck chair close
to hers. Then, smiling as he knew how to do, he apologized
for having to work on a new play instead of talking; and
he abstracted his attention. The flattered lady could be
calculated upon to keep intruders away for the rest of the
voyage.

Not many months after Shaw got back from Russia,
Charlotte wanted to go to South Africa for the winter.
The voyage was a success; they liked the climate; and

Shaw, who got a pleasure out of landscape, enjoyed the scenes. He liked driving, too. It gave him the illusion of working, combined with a rest from mental toil. As Charlotte did not drive, they had a chauffeur in England; but even there Shaw often took the wheel. He was quite a good driver in the ordinary way, but in a crisis he was no more to be relied on than he had been on bicycles when he was younger. He had learned to drive on an early car whose arrangement of pedals was different from that of the later ones, so that in an emergency he tended to stamp on the accelerator instead of the brake. At home in the Rolls, the chauffeur usually sat by him, alert to turn off the ignition when this happened. In Africa, his companion was unaware of his little foible, so that he did nothing when the car swerved out of control, dashed over a bank, through a barbed wire fence, down a ravine and up the other side before Shaw managed to get his foot off the wrong pedal and put it on the right one. Poor Charlotte, who was riding in comfort in the back as she always did, was thrown to the floor and battered by the heavy luggage. Her glasses were broken and the wire rims driven into her cheeks, her wrist was sprained, her back was bruised, and she had a wound in her shin which soon became infected and looked quite dangerous.

They canceled their arrangements and stayed where they were till Charlotte got better. After the first anxieties were over, Shaw did not mind. The climate was perfect, the bathing wonderful, and he had a new idea for a book. *The Adventures of a Black Girl in Search of God* takes the Black Girl through the various beliefs of men and leaves

The Shaws on their travels. At San Francisco airport, 1932.

her with an old philosopher, who is Voltaire, and an Irishman, who is Shaw. He tells her that he does not think God is completely made and finished. The Life Force is driving to express itself through trial and error, and it is men's job to help it find itself. "And he spat on his hands and went on digging," wasting not a moment of his time on earth.

In the following winter Charlotte was more ambitious; and they went right around the world, appearing briefly for the first and only time in America, landing in San Francisco and also spending one day in New York, where Shaw gave an address which was far from flattering at the Metropolitan Opera House. Next winter they were off to New Zealand.

Plays still poured out of him. The Malvern Festival found him vigorous when it came to rehearsal. The old juggler had his box of tricks, but the world had changed since his great days. The Malvern Play of 1931 had been entitled *Too True To Be Good* and for the first time attempted to take for its theme the modern generation. For a long while now Shaw had never met young people, except at Malvern or the Royal Academy of Dramatic Art, where he only saw them as pupils. He was out of sympathy with them, appalled by their manners, revolted by their untidy appearance and their eternal cigarettes, slightly contemptuous of the brash opinions which he had done so much to form. He perceived their energy and admired it, but was bewildered by a world no longer his own. *Too True To Be Good* has a hero, if one can call him that, who is a preacher, but has lost his message. He has outgrown his religion, his political system, his own strength of mind and character. He is utterly lost, and yet: "My gift has possession of me: I must preach and preach and preach no matter how late the hour and how short the day, no matter whether I have nothing to say." It is Shaw's verdict on the postwar generation, and yet also it is Nature's verdict on Shaw. It is the vengeance of Time on the preacher, the prophet humbled. His day is past, and yet he has to go on talking.

There was much need for someone to talk. The mid-thirties are the years when the world first learned to dread Hitler and hate the Nazi regime. It so happened that the Fabian Society, which was fifty years old in 1934, had established a series of lectures which were annually given in London. These too reached their fiftieth year, and it was tradition that Shaw delivered the concluding lecture. Accordingly, on this special occasion Fabians from out of town, many of them municipal or even Trade Union politicians, crowded the audience, together with Labour members of Parliament or the London County Council, professors from the London School of Economics, and students of liberal or radical views. It was an audience more socialistic and more politically minded than Shaw was likely to find elsewhere in England.

He did not waste his chance. Despite his age, he was still upright; and his voice was as clear as it had ever been. If they wanted to know what man he most admired in Europe, he told them, it was Hitler. And if they wanted to know why, they had only to look on his face. The expression on it was a scowl of discontent, and this expression was the only one which any intelligent man could wear when he looked on the state of Europe. He then developed his admiration of Hitler.

This might be witty, but it raised no laugh. In the Labour Party there was a strong pacifist group, among which many people were beginning to feel with infinite pain that the principles of a lifetime must be discarded. To such men, Hitler was not a joke, while praise of him was not a suitable subject for a Fabian lecture on a jubilee occasion. True to his practice, Shaw had sounded the note which would be most annoying.

In this way he came to the end of a long connection. The parting was decently veiled. Shaw was a life member of the society, and at eighty he was retiring from the platform in any case. He had always been forgiven as "that mad Irishman," but this time not all of the Fabians put aside their resentment. Officially nothing was said, but his day as a Fabian was over.

In 1938 with the situation in Europe growing ever more ominous, Shaw brought the dictators onto the stage in *Geneva,* setting Mussolini, Hitler, and Franco to defend themselves before the judge of the World Court at The Hague. The complaints of oppressed people — Jews and others — which have been the basis of the whole trial are soon forgotten. Shaw shuts his eyes to deliberate malice as if there were no such thing. The judge finds the dictators and the British liberal politician alike harmless — personally, that is. In foreign policy they are all equally scoundrels, since nationalism has for its object domination and for its instrument war. "There are a thousand

Shaw at his London flat in 1938.

good things to be done in your countries. They remain undone for hundreds of years; but the fire and the poison are always up to date." The indictment is perfectly true, yet it is too obvious that only the organization of Man now matters to Shaw. "Man is a failure as a political animal" is his verdict on Hitler, and he sneers at the unoffending Jew to get a laugh.

Bernard Shaw was never a man to pin down. One did not so easily come to an end of him. In 1939, a year after *Geneva*, he published a very different sort of play. *In Good King Charles's Golden Days* is more of a discussion than a drama. The action is almost nonexistent, and what there is of it has little bearing on the subjects discussed. Shaw has simply taken Charles II, who was an intelligent man and had his own laboratory, and brought him together with the great figures of his time — Isaac Newton, George Fox, the founder of the Quakers, Nell Gwynne, the actress, and Godfrey Kneller, the painter, together with his brother James and various ladies. They talk about the English and how to rule them, about what religion is, about whether science or art can come the closest to truth. Perhaps there is little that Shaw can say which he has not said already; yet he has steeped himself in the thought of the seventeenth century, a time when many of the things which troubled him were also called in question. *Good King Charles* is not just the old preaching; it is an intellectual effort which a younger man might have been proud to have made. It reflects also the wise and humorous outlook of a man who knows that answers to great questions are not simple, but that he must get along with other people who are apt to think they are. There is nothing sour about this play. It is rather the play which the author of *Saint Joan* might have been expected to write when he grew old.

1935–1950

The End of a Long Evening

In 1935, a Hungarian ex-actor arrived to see Shaw without an appointment and with little more cash than the small change in his pocket. Gabriel Pascal had been a rolling stone. He had even toured the Far East with puppet plays displayed in shadows on a screen. At the moment he was on his way to China, provided that Shaw would not allow him to produce a movie of *Pygmalion*. He had given himself somewhat less than a week to persuade an old man who had already turned down similar offers with far better financial backing. He actually gave Shaw a deadline. If he did not receive a contract by four o'clock in the afternoon on a certain day, he was off for the East. Promptly at four as Big Ben struck, a district messenger sent by the mischievous old man knocked at his door.

From the very first, Shaw had taken an intelligent interest in the cinema as a new art medium. It was not, however, until the appearance of the talking film that he would consider the reproduction of his plays as a possible question. When he did so, difficulties at once cropped up.

Owing to the techniques of movie making, he could not direct a dress rehearsal and be sure the play was produced as he had conceived it. In addition, the movie men insisted his plays must be cut.

They were not the only ones to take this view. The stage had always had trouble with Shaw's verbosity, and many were the arguments in which he had engaged. He insisted that no cuts be made by anyone but himself, on the grounds that other people cut out the serious parts and left the fooling. He then refused to cut at all and was known on some occasions to have had friends in the audience of a performance which he had not rehearsed himself going over the dialogue line by line to be certain that none of it was left out. When Lawrence Langner of the Guild Theater in New York brought over photographs of his production of *Heartbreak House,* Shaw put an indignant finger on the actress playing Hesione. "She's blond!"

Langner admitted it, but reassured him. It had been a great performance.

"What did you do about my lines on her dark hair?"

"Well, we sort of mumbled them," Langner said. "What would you have done?"

Shaw accepted this defense without demur. Anything was better than having an inexperienced hand tamper with his words.

Since this was his attitude, it is hardly surprising that only one of his major plays had been used as a movie, and that this had not been a success. *Arms and the Man* had come out in 1931, but it had been the work of an English

Shaw, discussing the filming of "Pygmalion," with Robert Morley,
Wendy Hiller, the star, Blanche Patch, and Gabriel Pascal, the producer.

company with more ambition than funds or experience.
To save money, it had been shot in Wales instead of the
Balkans; and it had not managed to make the slightest
stir. Gabriel Pascal's might have seemed an equally un-
promising speculation, but he did have some points in his
favor. In the first place, his ambition was the same as
Shaw's, namely to reproduce in a new medium the play
that Shaw had written, not to take it as the basis of a popular version, as he helped to do later on in *My Fair Lady*.
Secondly, Pascal had energy and initiative. The man
who could treat Shaw as he did and get what he wanted

had at least a chance of being successful in raising the money.

Pascal set about screening *Pygmalion* with enthusiasm, never hesitating to come to Shaw at every stage and talk over his plans. The result was, the old man soon took as much interest as Pascal. He actually was persuaded to write connecting scenes, so that the action might flow more smoothly than on stage. It was in this way that the garden-party scene which became later the climax of *My Fair Lady* came to be written.

Shaw did not go down to the studios during production, but he attended a lavish celebration on the occasion of the film's being launched, when he poked about behind the scenes to his heart's content, asking technical questions. The enormous success of *Pygmalion* encouraged him to give his consent to film versions of *Major Barbara* and *Caesar and Cleopatra*. He and Pascal were actually working on *Major Barbara* in 1939 when war broke out. To everybody's astonishment, Pascal was now so powerful that he had managed to persuade Shaw that the play must be shortened. In addition, the old man wrote sixteen fresh sequences for the film, though most of them had to be left out in the end because of its length. He even consented to appear in an introduction, fascinated as always by the process of being photographed, and presenting a perfect stage performance of himself.

Charlotte had not appeared when *Pygmalion* was launched. She had always hated the publicity which attended Shaw, and she scowled at photographers. In any case, however, she was beginning to feel old. In her middle seventies she had been glad to go around the world. By her eighties she had practically ceased to travel at all. She was having a great deal of pain in her back which was finally diagnosed as a crippling bone disease, incurable at her age. She became more and more bowed until finally she had to be lifted into a chair and was discovered crawling across the floor to get something she wanted.

In 1928, the building in which the Shaws had their London apartment was torn down. They had moved to a more modern one with a balcony, a view of the river, and service provided by the management. Between this and Ayot most of their lives were now spent. While Charlotte could still get about, the gardener often saw them walking around and around the garden at Ayot, counting the circles they made by leaving a pebble on a windowsill each time they passed it. Shaw, it is true, still strolled through the village; but Charlotte shrank from being stared at and preferred to get her exercise in the garden.

The house was still as well run as ever. In the thirties Charlotte had a jewel of a housekeeper, and the garden employed two men. Charlotte cared about her garden and gave orders about the flowers in the beds, which Shaw did not often notice. His attitude was perfunctory. He liked the place to be pleasant, took pride in eating home-grown garden produce, and let the gardener do what he really cared for, which included keeping bees and fantail pigeons. What Shaw most enjoyed was a little summer house which he put up to work in away from the telephone or other distractions. It was built to be revolved

so that it could always be warmed by the sun, an important point in England. It was soon obvious that Shaw did not care for the trouble of adjusting it and did not mind the cold. He let it stand as it happened to be, using it with perfect indifference, no matter which way the wind blew.

His furnishings were very simple: a wicker chair, a small table, a thermometer, and an alarm clock which he never heard to warn him about lunch. He was an adequate typist when he needed to be so, though he had to take his portable up to town for his secretary to change the ribbon.

In the afternoons he would rest, walk with Charlotte, or amble around Ayot St. Lawrence. The tiny village, which lay well off the main road, had no public utilities or transportation. The Old Rectory had a generator of its own for power and pumped its water with a gasoline engine. Most of the Ayot men were agricultural laborers, though some of the cottages were converted as time went on by commuters from London. For a long while nobody had taken much interest in the Shaws. According to his own account a local tradesman had replied in answer to inquiries: "He does something in Lunnon, I think, sir. But it isn't for *me* to ask him about his trade — now is it, sir?"

Apparently opinion changed when somebody or other saw a picture of a London street scene in the paper with a policeman actually holding up the traffic for Ayot's Mr. Shaw to cross the street. Whether it was true that after this episode he woke up to find himself a local celebrity,

Shaw turning his summer house. His suits are still all wool, and his shirt and tie likewise.

it was certainly the case that long before the thirties visiting dignitaries had been seen inquiring the way to the Old Rectory, and prowling reporters had infested Ayot St. Lawrence on numerous occasions. Shaw even changed the name of his house to "Shaw's Corner" because "The Old Rectory" was getting to be a considerable nuisance to the new one.

He had always been on good terms with his neighbors though they found him eccentric. One woman was walking home from work when she found Shaw sitting on a stile she had to cross, writing in his notebook. She said, "Please let me pass," but he ignored her. She repeated it loudly.

"Oh dammit, woman," exclaimed Shaw, "you've interrupted my train of thought and cost me a hundred pounds!"

"If you were a gentleman," she retorted, "you'd get off and let me by."

On the whole, however, he was mildly benevolent, made his contributions to the village fair or football club and helped largely in the restoration of the church. He did not even object to giving a public play-reading or a lecture to the rural women's club. He made an arrangement whereby every schoolchild in the village had a shilling's credit for candy at the local store on his birthday. When it came, however, to being told that it was his duty to do something directly for the school, old prejudice overcame him. He did not go so far as to refuse, but made inquiry whether there were already prizes given to the best-behaved boy and girl. Reassured on this point, he

promptly offered prizes to the worst-behaved, on condition that records be kept so that it could be established
whether the best or the worst children turned out better.
This handsome offer was refused, confirming what he had
always thought about schools — that they were essentially prisons where children were put to be out of the way
of the grownups, and where they were bribed not to be
a nuisance.

He was thoughtful of his neighbors in an imaginative
way. Mrs. Lyth, the postmistress, who was making out
on a very small stipend, had become a particular friend.
Shaw bought from her all the stamps he needed for his
vast correspondence; and though he was often in her tiny
general shop, he was careful never to buy his stamps in
person. He invariably wrote for them, signing the order,
which he knew that she could sell to autograph collectors for more than her profit on the stamps she sent him.
He had a photograph taken for her to make up postcards
of his new gate with "Shaw's Corner" written on it in
wrought iron. He even posed for a second postcard of
himself.

The Second World War, surprisingly, did not bring
many changes to the position of the amateur squire of
Ayot St. Lawrence. The second gardener went off to war,
as did some of the laborers from the cottages on the main
street. The places of those who went were filled with
evacuee children from London. Nobody, however, dared
to billet children at Shaw's Corner. The maids, being
elderly, had stayed. Charlotte required nursing. Presently
the secretary came down from London because of the

bombing. The place was undoubtedly a rambling old ark, but it was reasonably full. Nor was it feasable to board any children with such elderly people without sending a younger woman along to look after them.

The Shaw establishment was left alone, while Charlotte's condition grew worse by inexorable degrees. Earlier Shaw had said: "If Charlotte were on her deathbed, I know an infallible way of restoring her health. I'd simply go to bed and say I was dying." This did not work any more. He was everything that was patient and

Garden gate at Ayot St. Lawrence.

consoling, even moving his piano into the hall because she liked to hear him play and sing old favorites in the evenings as she lay in bed.

Ayot must have seemed strangely quiet and lonely, now that reporters were busy with the blitz and friends were unable to travel. Nancy Astor came when she could, and sometimes people met him at the local bar in the village so as to save Charlotte the strain of entertaining. Even Shaw's long intercourse with Sidney Webb was broken because neither could get about. Sidney had a stroke from which he partially recovered, but he never left his country house again. Then Beatrice died.

In 1943, Charlotte seemed a little better. The London blitz was over now; and he was able to take her up to the apartment so that the servants down at Ayot could have a vacation. The face of London was greatly changed, but he liked to wander about it and examine the places that he once knew. He was getting a little tottery, and friends worried because he would go out to walk in the blackout, confiding in a light raincoat to make him visible to autos or buses in the dark.

The housekeeper down at Ayot got ill, so that they could not return as they intended. Presently Charlotte grew so much worse that there was no question of going back. She had delusions that the flat was full of people, said she must complain to the manager. The place was expensive and they had a right to have it to themselves. He told her that she was getting better, but that her illness had made her clairvoyant. She was not losing her mind: these were real people. The only trouble was that

they were actually in Australia, or Oxford, or somewhere
else. The manager would not be able to see them. This
comforted her. A little while later she suddenly seemed
at peace again and well, the lines of worry all smoothed
out of her face, so that she reminded him once more of
how he had first seen her. In this peace Charlotte died,
leaving Shaw at eighty-seven with who knew how many
years to face without her.

He had never ceased to work. It was obvious to him,
as indeed it was to everyone else, that the state of Europe
and of England would prove to have been profoundly
altered by the course of World War II. Much depended
on making a more permanent settlement than had been
made after World War I. Accordingly in 1944 he published *Everybody's Political What's What,* in essence *The
Intelligent Woman* brought up to date and directed
toward the problem he had in mind. Alas, he was too old
for the task. It was not merely that he had said everything
before. Large chunks of *The Intelligent Woman* had transferred themselves almost unaltered into the new book.
Passages, too, were repeated more than once. The publishers were forced to do an editing job which was made
more difficult because when they crossed a paragraph out
on its second appearance, Shaw was apt to reinsert it somewhere else. After fearful efforts, *Everybody's Political
What's What* was finally published and hailed as the remarkable work that it was — for his age. Undoubtedly
there are gems of expression in it, while many things he
had said before would bear repeating. But the world had
ceased to look to Shaw for a new message.

His life settled down after Charlotte's death and was even in some respects easier, since the strain of her illness and the constriction of her loving care had been oppressive in the last years of her life. She left her money to a fund for improving the culture and manners of the Irish people which offended their bristling national pride — unnecessarily, since surely every nation needs improvement. Shaw's own fortune was more than he needed to keep his establishments up, despite the inflation of the war. No one, however, could convince him of this. When he was away at Malvern in the thirties, he would take his chauffeur along, so that the task of delivering the daily papers at Ayot was entrusted to the chauffeur's little girl, who was rewarded by a slice of the special cake they made for Shaw with plenty of nuts in it. Nuts were a luxury which the chauffeur's family could not afford; but when he asked Shaw for a raise, the wealthy old man replied with earnest conviction that his expenses were too great for him to grant it.

If he had always been mean, the staff would not have stayed; but he could be generous, too, and was personally pleasant. A Catholic housemaid was driven every Christmas to the midnight mass at Westminster Cathedral — in the Rolls. His excellent housekeeper proved willing to carry on when Charlotte died, merely insisting that he look over the household accounts at the end of the month. This gave him a chance to buy an adding machine, since he adored gadgets and did not stint himself of the few things he wanted. When he had to have new dentures at the age of ninety-one, he insisted on gold work, not only in the pair he intended to wear, but in those he had made to keep in reserve. He could afford it, he said with typical inconsistency.

In 1946, his ninetieth birthday brought him back into the news with a hundred telegrams, two regular sacks full of mail, and a siege of reporters. When a policeman was stationed at the gate to keep them out, one even tried to bribe the mailman to let him deliver the letters. Shaw did not care, and never had cared for these remembrances; but he had not failed to notice when he was seventy that he had received official congratulations from the German foreign minister, while the British government took no notice at all. How like the English! he had grumbled. It was indeed like them, as was the tolerance which had endured more criticism from him than any other government would have put up with. Typical also was the scramble of the papers to invade the privacy of the grand old man, treating his ninetieth birthday with more attention than they had done his works.

His personal prestige, however, was unchallenged. In 1947 Sidney Webb died. It was Shaw who insisted that the achievement of the Webbs be honored by the nation with burial of their ashes in Westminster Abbey among England's mighty dead. Thus Sidney and Beatrice Webb, incongruously unobtrusive, became one with the pageant of English history. For his part, with a flash of Irish independence, Shaw had other plans.

In 1949 the Labour government, establishing the welfare state as planned by disciples of Beatrice and Sidney, imposed a capital levy. Shaw panicked. He had never

Shaw in the garden at the age of ninety.

approved of taxing capital as though it were income, and no one could persuade him that he was not likely to go bankrupt. He would have to cut down! He decided to get rid of the London flat, which was now only used as an office for his secretary to work in. He did not in the least desire to have her move to Ayot, which would have bored her and forced him to be social when he wanted to be private. Eventually he decided to take a smaller, furnished apartment in which she could set up her office. All the contents of the apartment he had, including prompt copies of his works, annotated in his own hand, busts, portraits, presentation copies of books from well-known friends, manuscripts, and documents of all sorts were sold for what they could fetch in a hurry. Even two rugs which had been sent down to Ayot were judged too expensive to keep and returned to be sold.

At the age of ninety-two, he actually published the last of his full-length plays. *Buoyant Billions* is in essentials a farce, its characters reduced to puppets, "Firstborn," "Secondborn," and the like, its decor flavored for no particular reason with scenes fom the Far East. But still the old man talks on the old themes, and the play hung together well enough to run for a few weeks in London after being produced at the Malvern Festival. In his preface, he apologizes for what he has done:

> I can hardly walk through my garden without a tumble or two; and it seems out of all reason to believe that a man who cannot do a simple thing like that can practise the craft of Shakespear . . . Well, I grant all this; yet I cannot hold my tongue nor my pen. As long as I live I must write. If I stopped writing I should die for want of something to do.

Why he must write, he cannot tell. Such is his nature.

He goes back to Methuselah again and produces *Far-Fetched Fables*, which runs briefly through the development of Man from a twentieth-century human being to a thought vortex. In a long and rambling preface he tries to come to grips with the problem of how to test the abilities of mankind, stopping everywhere by the wayside to give brief summaries of his views on religion, social equality, education, medicine, diet and all the convictions or prejudices accumulated in his lifetime. His interest in himself deepens, and he publishes *Sixteen Self*

Splitting wood for exercise. Shaw in old age.

Sketches full of personal reminiscences. He descends to a rhyming guide to Ayot St. Lawrence — everything and anything because he has to keep on writing.

By now he looked extraordinarily old, his hair of a shining whiteness and his complexion baby-pink. He did not walk far any longer, but took his exercise by sawing wood or pruning the trees in the garden. On the whole, his health was very good. In his early eighties he had collapsed of severe anemia and had been pulled around, at Charlotte's insistence, by liver injections. He had put up with this outrage on vegetarian principles to please her and, once accustomed to the notion, had consented to take pills. He tired easily now, but he still on occasion could become the old public figure who felt it incumbent on him to entertain people by his brilliance.

He had made up his mind to leave his fortune for a project which interested him, but nobody else. He wanted a phonetic alphabet devised for the English language with some forty characters instead of twenty-six which should cover properly the actual sounds which English contains. Its advantages were that it would simplify spelling and be much quicker to write. He estimated that the saving in actual paper and ink would be enormous, not to mention in people's time. His idea was to offer a prize for such an alphabet and then to finance printing some books in it. Perhaps with such a start its obvious merits would drive our present alphabet out of existence. At all events, he was glad to leave his money to something positive and new. His interest in phonetics had lasted all his life, from his days in Ireland, through the writing of *Pygmalion,* and on to work between the two wars as chairman and guide of the British Broadcasting Company's committee for spoken English. Here experts submitted pronunciations of peculiar words, proper names, foreign words, and so forth, while the committee decided what to recommend. It had also been working on a standard pronunciation which would do for British and American radio speakers. Thus though people warned him that his will would prove impractical, he would not alter it.

On September 10, 1950, when he was ninety-four, he fell while trying to lop a dead branch from a tree in his garden, fracturing his thigh. He was taken to a hospital, where the reporters descended in a body, clamoring for news downstairs and even trying to climb up a ladder and through a second-story window.

Everything possible was done, but the old man was clearly cracking up. To a friend he said indignantly all this care was a waste of time. He was in hell, not a hospital. Why did he have to be washed and massaged and waked when he was asleep and asked why he could not sleep when he was awake? At least at home they would let him die in peace. He wanted to die!

They took him home as he desired at the beginning of October; and for four weeks he lay in bed, not showing much interest, only saying once when his secretary read him a letter, "I must write to him." The busy pen was still at last.

"I am going to die," he said finally with determination, and he lapsed into unconsciousness, never speaking or noticing anyone again until he died.

His ashes were mingled with Charlotte's at Ayot. His undistinguished house was left to the nation. There was an effort made to carry out his will; but it came to nothing, as he had been warned that it would. His money was divided between the Irish National Gallery of Art, which he had so often visited as a boy in Dublin; the British Museum, which had been his university, and his library and workroom; and the Royal Academy of Dramatic Art, where he had coached a generation of England's leading actors in his plays.

It is to be hoped that he rests quiet in his grave. Not

only were the provisions of his will thus set aside, but a
few years after his death his most popular comedy, *Pygmalion*, was transformed by a syndicate into *My Fair
Lady*, not only cutting about his sacred text, but actually
focusing on the romantic feelings which he mocked at
above all others. The enormous royalties accruing from
this musical went to swell his bequest to institutions whose
future would have been assured without it and which, he
felt, should be supported by the state. Surely for their
sake he never would have sacrificed a line of what he
had written. One may almost hear a voice from Ayot St.
Lawrence remarking, with a faint hint of brogue, that vandalism is all that anyone can expect from the English. With
the Americans, who are equally at fault, he has no quarrel.

Epilogue

IT IS PARTICULARLY hard to estimate the achievements of Bernard Shaw because they fall into two categories. We can read his imaginative works and try to form an opinion of their merit, comparing them, as he often did, to Shakespeare's, or to those of great contemporaries like Ibsen and O'Neill. To discuss them in this sense, however, seems beyond the task of a biographer, who has no business to tell his readers what to think, particularly if they happen not to have read all the works in question. A far more difficult task, and one which does seem appropriate, is to trace Shaw's influence on his own times, or, in other words, to see how he has indirectly affected ours. Shaw was a persistent "world-betterer," to use his own phrase. We do him a real injustice if we treat his plays merely as artistic expressions of the early twentieth century and compare them with other such expressions of mood. Nor can we ignore that side of his work which was not creative, merely remarking that though no doubt useful, it had only temporary value. Our century has not simply shaped itself, and Shaw has a place among those who made it what it is.

Shaw's work for the Fabian Society needs first to be considered because it was such a large part of his total activity. What the Fabian Society essentially did was to form itself into a school for those who perceived that society was not organized on principles of efficiency or justice. It is easy to criticize society in a general way, but far more difficult to find out exactly where things go wrong, suggest remedies, and master the technical steps involved in getting action. Now the moving spirits of the Fabian Society were unquestionably the Webbs. It was they who did the heaviest part of the research into the workings of the Poor Law, local government, and other subjects. It was they who founded the London School of Economics and *The New Statesman.* Sidney did the magnificent work for London University. Nevertheless, the influence of Shaw on the Fabian society was profound. In the early days while the society was forming itself, his directing influence was if anything greater than Sidney's, partly because he had more spectacular ideas, and partly because as long as Sidney was in the Colonial Office, Shaw had more time. Even when Sidney doubled himself by marriage with Beatrice, there was one function which he never took over from Shaw. Sidney's written style was deadly dull. In his early days he was adequate, even occasionally good, as a speaker; but later on he became inaudible and hardly tried to hold his audience. It was only natural that Shaw should become the Fabian propagandist.

The effect of *Fabian Essays,* of the other pamphlets written or edited by Shaw, as well as of his speechmaking at least once a week for nearly fifteen years, was profound. Opinion, in the days before radio, was formed by such means. The process was slower than it is to-day, but not dissimilar. It was undoubtedly due to Shaw that thoughtful minds were attracted by the Fabians and that the prestige of belonging to the society became great. If measured by the quality of the people whom it affected, the importance of the Fabian was tremendous.

Broadly speaking one may say of the Fabian Society that it provided both inspiration and practical plans for nearly all the major advances made in the field of social welfare in Great Britain during the first half of the twentieth century. Unemployment insurance, workmen's compensation, old age pensions, socialized medicine, and many other aspects of what we like to call the war on poverty are owing in large measure to Fabians, as well as more obviously socialistic measures, such as the nationalization of the British railways.

This is not to say that there were not other forces at work besides the Fabians, or other Fabians besides Shaw concerned in these matters. Nevertheless, when the great playwright was asked at the end of his lifetime whether his imaginative or his propagandist work was more important, Charlotte, who was never disposed to underestimate her husband's genius, voted for the propaganda. The fact that she could do so, or indeed that the question could be put at all, may serve to demonstrate the importance which informed people could attach to Shaw's Fabian work.

Whatever the final verdict may be, it is surely obvious that the influence of Shaw on his time was not exclusively political. Where he worked by himself, in his plays and his personal writings, he was constantly in advance of his age. The purpose of his comedies is to make us take a fresh look at old ideas or old values which we have long taken for granted. How widely his thought ranged we may see from a study of his prefaces, which are generally essays on a subject suggested to him by the play in question. One discusses the ethics and practical problems of censoring plays, one is on marriage laws, one on our credulousness about scientific miracles or medical knowledge, one is on family life, one on democracy, one on the Four Gospels. In every case, Shaw has something interesting to say. If it does not seem new to us, this generally means that our thinking has caught up with his. If so, we need not suppose he was never ahead of us. It is probable that he, even if only one among others, has enlarged our opinions.

This is what Shaw had in mind when he wrote comedy. One of the functions of comedy is to be amusing; another is to criticize the way things are. The subject of comedy may be as general as the stupidity of mankind; it may be as special as the conceit of a man who has got rich fast in a particular era. What really matters is that comedy is intellectual, tragedy emotional. King Lear's tragedy, for instance, might happen to any father in any age. It has nothing to do with the relation of parents to children in ancient Britain or in Shakespeare's day. Doolittle, Eliza's father in *Pygmalion,* appears grown suddenly rich and gives us a burlesque view of the very problem with which Eliza herself is concerned. What is the difference between lady and gentleman, flower girl and dustman? In Eliza's case it is accent, manners, and dress. In Doolittle's it is more vulgarly money. These comedy problems, however, are intellectual ones related to the values of a definite society. Shaw's comedies are written to make us think about these values.

An influence of Shaw's kind is hard to measure, even when it has been very real. A minor incident toward the end of Shaw's life may show that the effect of a fresh view can be a practical one. A criminal escaped from Parkhurst prison and was at large for some days. After a hue and cry he was recaptured and, in accordance with regular practice, put in chains. Shaw immediately wrote to the papers protesting the punishment, which was more deserved by the carelessness of the prison authorities than by the prisoner, who had been sentenced to be imprisoned — not to imprison himself. "The commonest instinct of decent sportsmanship, to put it no higher, insists on the sacred right of the prisoner to escape if he can." The point was a new one, but well taken. Public opinion supported Shaw, and chains for escape were abolished.

An instance of this kind can be noted, as can also the number of people who wrote to ask Shaw for advice. All the same, it is impossible to be certain where we should stand on many issues if Shaw had never existed. It may therefore be helpful to look at a slightly more concrete side of Shaw's achievement and try to estimate his contribution to the history of drama.

It would not be fair to say that all the dramatists who

were writing in London in the eighties and nineties were bad. On the contrary, the best of them were highly skilled technicians who had a certain amount to say. The most obvious criticism that we can make of them is that they accepted too readily certain limitations on drama, affecting both style and subject matter.

Most important of these was that the characters of drama should be all well-to-do, so that the economic pressures which dominate ordinary lives should not affect them. Drama was afraid of being sordid, so that it never came to grips with the world as it is. The problems with which it saw fit to deal were basically emotional ones. *The Second Mrs. Tanqueray*, the sensational drama which made Mrs. Pat's reputation, is about a man who determines to marry a woman with a past. The theme of the play was not that society has no right to hold her past against a woman who is living respectably now. *The Second Mrs. Tanqueray* is about the sufferings of a woman whose past catches up with her — as it must and will. She herself recognizes, and everybody else does, that she is unworthy of a happy future. We sympathize with her in the sense that we sympathize with Macbeth. She is a noble character gone wrong. The play is notable for the courage with which it insists that such a woman can be a noble character at all, but it never goes so far as to defend her.

In the field of comedy, *The Importance of Being Earnest* shows similar marked characteristics. The characters have no jobs or economic problems. Their entanglements are purely personal ones which are solved as they pair off. Oscar Wilde was almost exactly Shaw's age and brought up in Dublin, but he blossomed and faded in an earlier period. Thus though his witticisms mock the upper classes, these remain his sole concern. He takes them seriously because he puts nothing in their place, preferring to laugh at everything in his small world, rather than to enlarge it.

The dramatist who first burst out of this restricted area was not Shaw, but Ibsen, the Norwegian. His dramas seemed to explode with shattering force just because they were about real people and actual problems. Ibsen, however, was a poetic, emotional writer, essentially conservative. While his plays championed freedom, it was usually personal freedom. His characters wallowed in as much emotion as Paula Tanqueray, even allowing for the fact that their motives and problems were more realistic. They came to the same sort of violent end. A new note was struck by Shaw in 1886 when he threw over Archer's plot which, influenced by Ibsen and the new realism, had called for a young man's renunciation of his wife's money because the source of it was tainted. In Shaw's version, the young man speedily finds his own money is tied up in the same dubious venture. If he withdraws it, he may unwittingly put it out at interest to something viler still. There is no room for a noble attitude or even an emotional experience which leaves its mark. The young man is caught, and the problem now ceases to be what he does about the money. It is what our civilization does to him, how his good impulses have no outlet, how his tastes and qualifications, even his love affair, combine to trap him into accepting an unworthy situation.

In this way, Shaw took up the drama he had inherited from Ibsen and widened it to challenge not merely the faults of society, as Ibsen had done, but society itself. This was only possible, however, if he could widen the intellectual scope of drama, as opposed to its emotional content. Shaw's plays very seldom strew the stage with corpses. Laughter tends to take the place of the great emotional scene, wit of heroism, even farce of plot. There is plenty of cut-and-thrust, but it is all verbal as Undershaft fights for the soul of Barbara, or John Tanner duels with Ann. Excitement is produced as characters battle over principles and ideas. Occasionally Shaw will produce a play like *Getting Married* in which nothing happens at all, so that the entire action concerns itself with what different types of people think about marriage. *Getting Married* is not one of Shaw's best plays, but it would have to be considered in any short list of his most typical ones, precisely because he has in this case abandoned the traditional construction of drama, so that he gives us nothing but his own original contribution, namely the drama of ideas.

To say that the drama of ideas belongs peculiarly to Shaw does not begin to measure his greatness as a dramatist, since he had other qualities of wit, imagination, style, and sympathy, for which he is justly admired. It does, however, give a good impression of his impact on his times. Any play that has been written after Shaw need not concentrate on making us feel an experience deeply if it prefers to make us see an idea clearly instead. Shaw has demonstrated that the one is not more thrilling than the other. Even more obviously he has shown that a combination of the two can be matchless. In fact, he has almost moved the serious theater into the place occupied by the pulpit long ago in the days when sermons were close-reasoned theological arguments, providing intellectual food for the coming week.

The influence of this new kind of preaching was vastly extended because Shaw was the first playwright who gave serious thought to the problem of getting his plays read. The famous prefaces — extra sermons in themselves — the careful stage descriptions and directions were all ideas of his. Before him, printed versions of a play were never sold except in batches to some group that wished to put on a performance. Shaw's plays, however, were read and widely discussed, occasionally even before they had been produced on the stage. They penetrated to places and people who never saw a theater. The ideas in them were challenging enough to make many reexamine old concepts which they had long taken for granted. Even timid persons ceased little by little to see any harm in thinking things over and occasionally adopting a new view. The twentieth century, in other words, had started its rejection of many of its standards.

It is hard to say whether we are better off for the revolution in thought and morals with which Shaw had so much to do. Not every change in the first half of the century was due to him; indeed with many he had no sympathy. But whether developments have been good or not, we can say one thing about them. There is only one way to go through history, namely forward. It is a wise man who looks at the past, or even the present with critical eyes, provided that his plans for the future be not spoiled by selfishness, faintheartedness, or lack of scruple. Of such failings we may acquit a man who strove consistently to better his world and asked no reward, save to be worn out in service before he was discarded.

Shaw at work in his summer house.

Suggested Reading List of Plays

Widowers' House (1892)
Arms and the Man (1894)
Candida (1895)
The Devil's Disciple (1897)
Caesar and Cleopatra (1898)
Man and Superman (1903)
Major Barbara (1905)
The Doctor's Dilemma (1906)
Androcles and the Lion (1912)
Pygmalion (1913)
Heartbreak House (1919)
Saint Joan (1923)
The Apple Cart (1929)

Movies

Major Barbara
Caesar and Cleopatra
Pygmalion

Recordings

Don Juan in Hell 2-Col OSL-166
Saint Joan 3-Vic LOC-6133
Letters to Ellen Terry Caed 1108